DISABLED READERS
Insight, Assessment, Instruction

DISABLED READERS
Insight, Assessment, Instruction

Edited by
DIANE J. SAWYER
SYRACUSE UNIVERSITY

INTERNATIONAL READING ASSOCIATION
800 Barksdale Road Newark, Delaware 19711

INTERNATIONAL READING ASSOCIATION

Copyright 1980 by the
International Reading Association, Inc.

Library of Congress Cataloging in Publication Data
Main entry under title:

Disabled readers.
  Includes bibliographies.
  I. Reading — Remedial teaching. 2. Reading disability.
I. Sawyer, Diane J.
LB1050.5.D57   428'.4'2   79-17153
ISBN 0-87207-490-0
Second Printing, December 1985

Contents

The International Reading Association attempts, through its publications, to provide a forum for a wide spectrum of opinion on reading. This policy permits divergent viewpoints without assuming the endorsement of the Association.

Foreword

In the past fifteen years there has been a tremendous degree of interest in, and concern for, those youngsters suffering with reading disability. Difficulty in school probably is the single, most immediate reason for children's being referred to child psychiatric clinics and child therapists. Unfortunately, all too often the children are approached with a unitary orientation so that extremely important aspects of their unique reading disabilities are ignored. There is certainly no one etiology for reading disorders. Rather, reading problems can be caused by any number of a multiplicity of factors, all of which may be highly interrelated.

Many different professionals are involved in working with children with reading disabilities. However, there is a tendency for each professional discipline to look at this serious problem through its own window of specialization. This tendency often obscures vital factors which may contribute to, or at least exacerbate, the basic difficulty. And complicating the entire picture is the fact that parents of children suffering with severe reading disabilities are ripe targets for any party who offers the panacea. The tragic reality is that the field has become ripe pickings for anyone who wants to capitalize on the sufferings of parents bewildered by the multiplicity of explanations offered to them. Therefore, it becomes increasingly important for the educator to become better aware of the controversial nature of many of the diagnostic strategies and multiple intervention techniques.

In this volume on the disabled reader, the editor makes no pretense that the discussions cover the entire range of issues in this controversial field. But Diane J. Sawyer has wisely limited her selection of papers in such a way that there still remains a significant representation of articles dealing with the nature of some reading difficulties, of those concerned with the assessment and diagnosis of reading problems, and of those that offer specific suggestions for both habilitation and rehabilitation.

Dr. Sawyer is also to be commended for selecting authors who have something important to say and who are able to communicate their ideas to the reader. The volume's focus is on helping the teacher to understand and to help the child who experiences reading disability. Many of us look for simple solutions. The task of dealing with reading problems is quite intricate; but the contributors to *Disabled Readers* do not hesitate to present their ideas forcefully, unequivocally, and clearly.

Increasingly, as our schools have become sensitized to the concept of "learning disability," there has been the tendency to forget that learning disabilities do not represent a homogeneous group of children but, in fact, a heterogeneous population. Too frequently, one forgets that the vast majority of children who are classified as learning disabled have, as their major presenting symptoms, difficulty in learning to read. Reading can be one of the most troublesome, yet most important, skills in school. A knowledge of reading is necessary for the mastery of almost every school subject; more children fail certain grades because of reading difficulties than for any other reason. It becomes extremely important, therefore, that teachers working with "learning disability" children acquire the competencies needed for dealing with reading problems.

The International Reading Association should be commended for bringing out this important volume at this time. Readers should take advantage of the many insights presented here. The ideas and strategies discussed in this book should help all of us avoid unnecessary frustration, disillusionment, and apathy in our efforts to reach children.

JULES C. ABRAMS

Introduction

The papers included in this volume have been prepared by practitioners at the various levels within the profession from public school, community, and university settings. The ideas presented have developed in the context of day to day contact with disabled readers, their teachers, and their families. It is hoped that, through this volume, the range and depth of experiences each of the contributors brings to a consideration of reading difficulties will modify and extend the basic issues to be considered in instructional planning and program development for disabled readers.

The papers have been grouped into three sections. Part one includes those which offer insights into the nature of some reading difficulties as well as into the personality and interpersonal dynamics of the reading disabled. Part two includes papers which describe various procedures for skill assessment, kindergarten through secondary school. One paper discusses how the process of psychoeducational evaluation can serve the dual purpose of pupil assessment and staff inservice. Section three includes papers which offer specific suggestions for instructional practices in developing reading proficiency, including work with visually or auditorily impaired students.

While we hope the papers in this volume will contribute to understanding, identifying, and planning for disabled readers, we must emphasize that the areas touched upon represent only a small sample of the issues and points of view related to the study of reading difficulties.

DJS

PART ONE

*Some Insights into Concomitant Aspects
of Reading Difficulties*

Perceptual Bases for Reading Difficulties

Diane J. Sawyer
Syracuse University

The act of reading, whether at the levels of decoding and word recognition or at sophisticated levels of comprehension, requires the extraction of information from the printed page. That information is analyzed and compared with previously stored information—information accumulated as a result of prior experiences with reading and a myriad of other types of activities. Associations are made which permit or yield such products as letter-sound recognition, word-name recognition, and the recognition of meaning at any of several levels— word, phrase, sentence, passage, chapter, book.

The kinds of information extracted during reading are varied, not bound exclusively to the physical page and the ink marks it displays. Rather, the pattern of ink marks is actively searched for cues (an outward directed search) which will prompt an inward directed search of information stored in the memory banks. In a task of letter-sound or word-name recognition, the visual search of the page ferrets out important letter or word features such as relations between lines and curves (m, v), directions of lines or curves (d, b), position of lines or curves with respect to the line of print (P, q), shape of word, length of word, and so on. The features detected are then used to initiate a search of the parts of memory devoted to the storage of information concerning the pairings of letter and word forms with the acoustic or sound features of letters and words experienced. When the inward search locates a form whose features are judged to match with the features selected as important from the page of print, it is possible for the reader to produce a verbal response such as "buh" if the task requires letter-sound recognition, or "want" if the task requires word-name recognition.

The visual search of the page considers or takes into account both features of letters, words and phrases *and* the conventions of text presentation. Experiences with print have taught us to use these conventions as road maps for getting through a page of print with minimum confusion but with maximum potential for achieving a clear impression of the message presented. At the beginning stages of reading, such conventions include lines, paragraph indentations, and headings or titles. The line convention requires left to right attention in the sampling of letter and word or phrase features. The line edges also serve as signals for beginning (at the end of a line) and ending (at the beginning of the next line) the top to bottom progress through a page of print.

Headings or titles very early come to be viewed as statements about the stories being read and apparently serve to mobilize the visual search systems by establishing a kind of "set of expectations" for the ideas and, therefore, the words and features readers are likely to encounter as their eyes meet the print. If the story is going to be about dressing up for Halloween, the inward directed search of memory, as described earlier, is likely to be facilitated if general and specific prior life experiences are called to mind before the outward directed search of the visual display is begun. The eyes will be directed more specifically; the search will follow more closely an hypothesis test model—seeking out information features which confirm or deny expectations of what might be found on the page. A reading experience so directed is likely to be more efficient, with fewer false starts. It is also likely to be fluent, with a higher degree or level of meaning abstracted overall because the energies devoted to the task were not split initially. Without such a set, more careful visual sampling for word recognition is likely to be required as the reader seeks to identify the general theme or topic and setting as well as abstract the relevant vocabulary, ideas, and details necessary to *construct* an impression of the overall message. This argument also supports the use of a directed reading activity in reading class or the use of study guides and systematic preview as approaches to independent reading in content text.

As readers become more skilled they encounter still other print conventions to which they must learn to respond appropriately. More advanced conventions include print presented in column form; captions as descriptions of pictures, graphs, and diagrams; and footnotes for explication or documentation. Efficient, skilled readers know to use these conventions of print presentation to their advantage in constructing as clear and as well organized an impression of the message presented, as is possible. Less knowledgeable readers fail to use these assists or use them inefficiently and actually become confused by them. Maturing readers must be taught how to integrate information available in the text as a result of the various print conventions if the outward directed perceptual search and the inward directed cognitive search and synthesis activities, which comprise the reading act, are to become increasingly efficient. To become efficient they must be purposefully organized.

The printed page also contains cues to meaning. These cues are presented visually. They too are ink marks on the page, but the reader's response to these cues must involve higher order associations. One example of such special features of the visual display is the letter *s*. When *s* begins the word *sun*, the reader's response need simply be at the level of association between visual symbol and acoustic or sound representation. But when *s* appears at the end of the word *cats*, a shift in the inward directed search systems must occur. The appearance of an *s* at the end of a word may signal a modification of word meaning. The word must be understood now to be made up of two parts, the category label for an animal *and* the marker to indicate or specify plurality or number.

In certain situations, the letter *s* signals meaning but in other cases it does not. The outward directed search of the page must be alert to these special features of the print form of language if the reader is to make meaningful distinctions between and associations with such words as *stand/canvas/spaces, run/ran, led/lead,* or *edifice/commented.*

The examples provided above show that in some situations letters or groups of letters signal phonemic or sound level associations, but in other situations those same letters or groups of letters must signal morphemic or meaning level associations. The visual search system must be guided to some extent then by the reader's knowledge of the conventions and structure of spoken language at the word and phrase level, for it is these conventions of oral language communication that spelling conventions attempt to designate or specify. In turn, awareness of the kinds of visual signals suggesting modifications of meaning within a word permits greater accuracy in the construction of the meaning of the message presented on a page.

Constructing a Message from Information Perceived

Throughout this paper, thus far, I have referred to *extracting* information from print and constructing the message in the reader's mind. It is important at this time to note that is how I understand the reading process to proceed. The mind is a storehouse of information about previous experiences in the world. The mind gathers in this information through the sensory input systems—vision, hearing, touch, taste, smell, and muscular sensations. The accuracy of the information stored—that is, how clearly the information received actually describes the world as it exists—is dependent in part upon the quality of functioning or level of efficient function which each sensory input system is capable of achieving. In part, accuracy is also dependent upon the ability of the brain to coordinate, organize, and integrate the information coming in as a result of experiences in the world and involves several of the sensory input systems in combination. The following might serve as examples of how information coming to us from different sensory systems might be coordinated by the brain to shape and reshape our understanding of and responses to the real world.

A sunny day, if viewed through a window, gives only an impression of light. But if one walks outside on a sunny day one gets an impression of light in combination with temperature so that the potential for accuracy in describing the day as "mild" or "warm" or "comfortable" or "startling" is increased as a result of integrating information coming in through two sensory systems in combination; information of two different kinds is extracted from the experience by the visual system and the skin's surface. The brain integrates both types of information and constructs an *impression* of reality. One person might describe the day as "sunny but cold," another might describe it as "sunny and mild," and a third as "glorious."

The differences in the descriptions offered suggest another important consideration in understanding the process of message construction, whether related to experiences in the physical world or to experiences with print. The message constructed reflects one's *impression* of reality, and those impressions are likely to be more or less different from person to person as a result of the type of previous experiences and the quality and quantity of those experiences. A Syracusan, like myself, is prone to describe a sunny day as "glorious" regardless of temperature since, statistically, we have so few sunny days each year. But a Californian or Floridian is more likely to describe a sunny March day in Syracuse as "brutally cold" and completely ignore the visual information portion of the experience. The brain has a tendency to select what of the incoming sensory information is important. What is selected as being important is, in part, a result of maturation and previous experiences. Further, what is selected is also a result of the dependability of the various input systems to search out and receive information.

If we consider the contribution to message construction of previous experiences and the relative ability or inability of sensory input systems to supply the brain with accurate information about the world, we can begin to understand the role of perception in reading whether we describe reading as word recognition (labeling) or as the apprehension of meaning.

The Effect of a Neurological Disability on Reading Performance

I once had the opportunity to work with a nine year old boy who suffered from cerebral palsy. The child had never had the use of his limbs; he was confined to a wheelchair and though he could move his arms and hands he did not have sufficient control to feed himself. The boy demonstrated average intelligence and was being taught to read. He evidenced two kinds of problems related to his reading. First, he had difficulty keeping his place while he read. The muscles controlling the movement of his eyes were also spastic. It was, therefore, difficult for him to move his eyes smoothly across a line of print. A sudden muscle jerk would interrupt his progress across a line and he would subsequently find his eye targeted on a line above or below the one he had been fixed on prior to the eye jerk. Reading was hard work for Sam. It required a great deal of energy and determination to make his eyes function as reasonable searchers of information on a printed page. Reproducing his reading materials so that the type size was large and the spaces between words and between lines were two or three times greater than normal helped Sam to cope better with the inconveniences of the spasms during reading. We couldn't improve the function of Sam's visual system, but we could adjust the material in such a way that he could more effectively use the visual abilities he did have.

Sam also had a problem with reading comprehension. He sometimes had difficulty grasping the humor, excitement, or danger of a situation being described. Sam had developed the ability to associate visual symbols with stored acoustic information—he could pronounce most words he met. Sam had developed a sufficient knowledge of the form and structure of spoken language to be able to interpret meaning shifts signaled at the level of the morpheme, as discussed earlier. But when we explored Sam's understanding of the world as reflected at the word level, some interesting deficits were discovered. Sam tended to have very literal and relatively superficial meanings he associated with rather critical kinds of words. To Sam, a slippery surface was simply "smooth"; something rough was "kind of scratchy." Sam really could not grasp the sense of a description of the fun children were having slipping and sliding on pond ice. Nor could he grasp the concern Mrs. Brown must have felt as she carried her bags of groceries down a slippery sidewalk. Neither could Sam fully understand the kind of play that leads children to develop control over their bodies, and, therefore, the ability to consciously control slipping and sliding in such a way as to make a game of it. Sam would be able to construct only very superficial impressions of the messages intended to be conveyed by authors, in some instances incorrect impressions, until and unless the adults in Sam's world undertook creative approaches to help him develop integrated sensory impressions at the level of *concept* formation, rather than distilled verbal labels or definitions, for the words he was able to pronounce when he met them in print.

The Process of Perception

Perception is an information gathering process. It involves the selection of information, judged pertinent and valuable to the task at hand, from the vast array of information present in the environment at any given time. Gibson (1) defines perceptual learning as "an increase in the ability to extract information from the environment, as a result of experience and practice with stimulation coming from it." Difficulties in acquiring the ability to read can occur as a result of a mismatch between a child's ability to extract and organize appropriate information through which to know and understand the world and the information processing demands of the reading act at the perceptual level.

The human mind learns about the world as a consequence of sensory, motor, and linguistic experiences in the environment. The quality and quantity of these experiences are dependent upon the circumstances or situation into which a given infant is born. The quality and quantity of information a given individual abstracts from those experiences is a result of the interaction among specific genetic endowment, physical and emotional well-being.

Maturation and Development of the Perceptual Systems

Among those characteristics which each of us inherits at the moment of conception are 1) a specific potential for intellectual functioning and 2) a time ordered program regulating the rate of maturation possible for perceptual abilities and other central process functions.

These perceptual and cognitive growth potentials are uniquely individual. Variability is seen from person to person even within families. In addition, the realization of this potential for any individual may be limited as a result of such complications as illness, disease, or injury during either the prenatal, birth or early childhood periods. Inadequate opportunities for the exploration of or stimulation in the environment might also specifically affect growth and development within the central nervous system during the critical growth period of the preschool years and serve to limit achievement of one's full perceptual and cognitive growth potentials. The case of Sam is offered as one example of how physical limitations may inhibit the realization of genetic potential. But there are other children who also have perceptual difficulties but not the outward physical characteristics that help make us sensitive to the possibility of their existence.

When children inherit very slow rates of physical maturation, we see small-for-age children who are not as well coordinated as their kindergarten or first grade schoolmates. It is easy to understand the kinds of problems such children might encounter in school because we can see their relative immaturity and can anticipate the possibility that they may experience fatigue more readily than others and may have greater difficulty learning to manage a pencil. The ramifications for school performance of slow maturation of the perceptual systems are less easy to anticipate. For the most part this is true because we cannot see directly the level of perceptual maturity achieved. We can only observe learning behavior which might suggest relative perceptual maturity. Unfortunately, we sometimes misinterpret the behavior and label children mentally retarded, unmotivated, or even emotionally disturbed, when in reality the children's levels of perceptual functioning are inadequate to meet the usual demands school type tasks make on their perceptual systems. If the children's perceptual development is simply lagging behind that of their age-mates, the potential is good for their eventually being able to meet the demands of school tasks. If, instead, perceptual abilities for a given child are not on a par with age-mates, due to damage or dysfunction within or between the systems, the

Sawyer

prognosis for school achievement is very poor unless s_
modifications of school demands can be made.

Whatever the cause of perceptual anomalies might be, the
that such anomalies might exist generally becomes apparent wh.
children encounter reading instruction. As was discussed earlier, the acι
of reading requires the association and integration of information
previously received and organized and stored, with the features of print
being selectively picked up through the visual system during the reading
act. Therefore, all aspects of perceptual function are called into play
during the reading act.

The Components of Perceptual Processing

Generally, the components of perceptual processing are
understood to include receptive functions, associative functions, and
memory functions. Receptive functions are those which are specifically
responsibile for taking in information and might be thought of as those
aspects of vision and hearing, for example, which are commonly
labeled acuity. Associative functions include those abilities which
permit us to understand what is being received. For example, if a
teacher holds up a picture of a tiger and at the same time says, "This
animal is a cat," children are able to distinguish the characteristics of the
animal shown and understand that the teacher wants them to think of
this animal as a kind of cat. Associative abilities must be able to operate
effectively both within and across the receptive sensory input modes.
Memory aspects of perceptual functioning include the abilities to make
same/different discriminations as well as the ability to store
information about differences between items and the ability to recall
that information at will.

Case Profiles

Perhaps the clearest possible way to demonstrate how slow
maturation or damage or dysfunction of one or more perceptual
systems, *or* how the ability to integrate information across two or more
perceptual systems, might result in reading difficulties is to share some
profiles of children seen at the Syracuse University Reading Clinic.
Each of these children was referred for an evaluation at the reading
clinic because of markedly poor achievement in reading. Each child
demonstrates a kind of perceptual processing problem which is believed

nsible for poor reading achievement. For some maturational lag associated with one or more of is responsible for the behaviors observed and the oblems encountered. In at least one case, and ossible that brain damage is responsible for the ...enced.

Jimmy

Jimmy was a second grader in a suburban Syracuse school district. Jimmy had a history of delayed speech, special speech therapy since age three, and difficulties in school achievement since school entrance. At the time of evaluation at the reading clinic, Jimmy had had much special assistance in school, especially in reading, but had achieved only rudimentary word recognition skills, and those not yet automatically applied.

Testing and observation indicated that Jimmy could receive information in the brain through any and all of his sensory input systems. At the time of testing, Jimmy's speech was intelligible, though some articulation difficulties were still in evidence. Jimmy was able to repeat words and short sentences when asked but had some difficulty determining whether two pronounced words, such as *tub* and *tug*, were the same or different. He also had difficulty repeating sentences of eight or more words and difficulty following directions when more than two separate actions were required. Jimmy had mastered the association among the sounds of consonants and blends and digraphs and their visual forms, but he had not yet mastered the operation in reverse (give the name of the letter for a sound heard at the beginning of a word). Jimmy had great difficulty spelling. Besides producing letter reversals (*d* for *b*) and confusing voiced/voiceless consonants (*pat* for *pad*), Jimmy would forget the sequence of sounds he was trying to write down when the words were longer than three letters. For example, he wrote *ska* for smoke and *spe* for strap. Jimmy also found it difficult to rhyme words and to hear the sounds in the middle of words.

It was concluded that Jimmy was experiencing difficulty in reading achievement because his auditory perceptual abilities were not sufficiently mature to meet the demands of typical second grade reading/spelling activities. This conclusion of maturational lag in the auditory perceptual system was drawn for the following reasons:

1. Jimmy did receive auditory stimuli in the brain.
2. Jimmy did not begin to speak until he was nearly three and his

speech at that time was unintelligible. By the age of eight, when we saw him for a reading evaluation, both his communication units and his articulation were nearly on a par with his age-mates. Such a developmental profile of speech acquisition suggested early difficulties with the association aspects of auditory perceptual function. The fact that abilities in this area improved as evidenced by adequate language use later, suggested that the early difficulties were due to slow maturation rather than damage or dysfunction in the system.

3. Jimmy still exhibited some difficulty in the areas of auditory discrimination and memory. However, his ability to master some of the sound-symbol associations, to follow two stage directions, to repeat seven word sentences and to separate out beginning and ending sounds of C-V-C words suggested a level of maturation for these abilities which was approximately on a par with average five or six year olds. He had shown improvement in all of these skills over the previous three years and, again, slow development of related auditory abilities was suggested as the reason for both his past progress and current deficiencies.

In light of Jimmy's level of auditory perceptual abilities and the increasing demands for independent reading as the principal means for gaining information as Jimmy progressed through the elementary grades, the following adjustments of the school program were recommended:

1. That Jimmy's ability to learn through listening be captialized upon in his classroom but that independent worksheet or workbook activities or silent reading in texts (other than the reading of pictures) be virtually eliminated.

2. That decoding instruction be focused on developing a recognition vocabulary of "personal," highly meaningful words and also on the analysis of words according to phonograms or clusters which pair the medial vowel with a consonant (*ot, at, it*), since such a pairing tends to help in the recognition of the regular sounds of the vowels.

In essence, the school was urged to play down Jimmy's difficulties in acquiring reading proficiency. Nonprint approaches to learning the content and concepts of the various subject areas were to be emphasized. While reading instruction was to continue, parents and teachers were cautioned that progress still might be slow. Adult anxiety over such slow progress might serve to hinder more than to help. Severely limited ability to learn via print was not to be an acceptable reason for withholding education.

Tim

Tim was a very bright, verbal ninth grader. Despite intensive special reading instruction beginning in second grade, Tim was still unable to read even second grade material with any degree of fluency. Many different approaches to reading instruction had been tried over the years, but none had yielded more than short term gains despite intensive instruction over long periods. At fifteen, Tim was hostile and verbally aggressive. His anger was directed toward some teachers, who, because he was so verbal and seemed so bright, ridiculed him. They accused him of laziness and of using reading difficulty as an excuse to get out of work. He was also angry with teachers who tried to help him learn to read because "They promise you things and then don't deliver." Mostly Tim was disgusted with himself because he had not been able to learn to read and, to Tim, being able to read meant being able to be a worthwhile person. Tim fell back on his strength in verbal diversionary tactics to conceal his inadequacies and to protect himself from further hurt. In doing so he became obnoxious and was even more isolated.

Examination of Tim's medical and developmental history showed normal development in all areas until the age of eighteen months when he became ill with spinal meningitis. During that time, Tim ran temperatures of 105+ for nearly ten days and was unconscious for several hours during the course of the fever. When Tim returned home from the hospital, it was apparent that he had lost his previous speech abilities. Subsequent speech development was slow and his communication efforts were unintelligible at the time he entered kindergarten. Intensive speech therapy over the next three years resulted in nearly perfect articulation and exceptionally fluent production. Unfortunately, similar gains in reading acquisition were never achieved. The possibility is suggested that brain damage might account for Tim's limited progress in reading. It appears that initial difficulties in the auditory system were overcome with maturation and training, but the specific interhemispheric capacities necessary to associate the symbol with the acoustic representation had not responded similarly. Tim's overwhelming difficulties in retaining either whole words or sound symbol associations despite fluent oral language and good reasoning skills suggest the possibility that the illness in infancy was responsible for some neurological damage which specifically limits reading acquisition. Tim has great difficulty producing controlled, legible letter forms. Capacities necessary to achieve visual-motor integration also appear to be involved.

Academically it appears that Tim can learn if requirements for reading and writing are circumvented. At the time of testing, however, his level of anxiety concerning school success was too high to allow Tim to open himself to learning. Professional counseling and unusual action on the part of school personnel seemed essential if Tim was to succeed in breaking down the defenses he had created to protect himself against continued failure.

Beth

Beth was a six year old who had just completed a year of kindergarten at the time of testing. Negligible academic achievement, coupled with evidence of perceptual-motor difficulties and a borderline full scale IQ (78) on a WISC administered by the school psychologist, led to the recommendation that Beth be placed in a class for the educable mentally retarded.

Testing at the reading clinic was conducted in the presence of Beth's parents as Beth cried and refused to take any test unless her parents were present. Even with them present, Beth refused to take any test requiring the use of machines, such as the vision and hearing screening tests, as well as other more school related tasks. Of the tests completed, Beth exhibited overall strength in auditory perceptual abilities but general deficiences in the area of visual-motor, fine motor, and gross motor coordination. In these areas, her performance was on a par with children two or three years younger than Beth. She had difficulty moving her eyes smoothly, both across a line of print and in sweeping from one line of print to another. Her ability to copy designs was very poor and some of her errors were consistent with a pattern typically described as suggestive of brain damage. On two different intelligence tests—Stanford-Binet and Peabody Picture Vocabulary Tests—which tapped primarily verbal abilities, Beth achieved IQ scores well within the normal range. On the Gesell Developmental Test, Beth's performance suggested a developmental age of approximately one year below her chronological age. Several prereading abilities appeared to be well developed. These included auditory discrimination, auditory blending, and visual perception of position in space as well as spatial relations.

Beth was an exceptionally shy child who at the age of six evidenced some specific visual perceptual and visual-motor integration difficulties. During testing by the school psychologist, these factors combined led to performance that suggested a profile of mental retardation. Under optimal test conditions provided in the reading clinic, her performance suggested the possibiity of either developmental lag specifically affecting visual-perceptual functions and visual motor integration or minimal brain damage affecting those same functions. At the age of six, it is very difficult to speculate about the relative potential for maturation to overcome perceptual anomalies of low magnitude.

It was recommended that Beth be placed in a class for the learning disabled where specific programs might be developed to meet her needs or that she be retained in kindergarten and placed with a teacher whose program stressed gross motor development, perceptual-motor skills, and sensory-motor integration. If slow maturation was at the core of Beth's problems, training and time would yield gains in visual perceptual function; if brain damage was the cause, her specific deficits would be even more readily identifiable in subsequent years.

Summary

Reading requires the extraction of information from the printed page and the active construction of the message the author intended to convey. Our sensory input systems gather firsthand information which permits us to know the world around us. Our perceptual systems analyze, organize, and store this information for us. In consort with our conceptual or thinking abilities, our perceptual abilities permit us to understand, question, and act on our experiences as well as interact in the world. When the level of perceptual function possible is inconsistent with the demands being made for its use, individuals' abilities to act upon their environment are impaired. The four students profiled in this paper exemplify discrepancies we might find in any classroom. Because the act of reading involves nearly all aspects of perceptual and cognitive abilities functioning cooperatively, perceptual anomalies are likely to effect slow or severly limited progress in reading acquisition. If teachers and parents understand that such might be the case, a more flexible approach to instructional goals and methods might be employed. At the same time, such an awareness should lead to the assessment of perceptual and cognitive abilities, as well as reading skills, in an attempt to locate the possible source of slow achievement in reading. Failure to progress in reading might signal the need to develop basic perceptual skills. Exclusive emphasis on reading skill development in such cases could yield a frustrating and defeating experience for all concerned.

Reference
1. Gibson, E.J. *Principles of Perceptual Learning and Development.* New York: Appleton-Century-Crofts, 1969, 3.

The Disabled Adolescent Reader

Jean F. Rossman
East Lynne, Connecticut, High School

The phrase *disabled adolescent reader* consists of three graphic words. As reading teachers we may immediately seize upon the word *reader,* testing pupils' skills to discover their academic deficiencies. Then, when pupils still fail to read adequately, we focus upon the first word, *disabled.* We look for auditory or visual defects, for physical or psychological disabilities which might be corrected. In this discussion, I would like to look at the middle word to ask whether in the nature of *adolescence* itself, and the adolescent experience in contemporary culture, there are further clues as to what must be done to help the disabled adolescent reader.

Defining Adolescence

A myriad of research books has sought to define adolescence and to describe the experience of teenagers. But when I survey this literature, what generalizations can I find that are worth repeating here or that can be applied in our efforts to assist one specific disabled reader? Tanner (5) points out that physiologically the adolescent has not changed significantly in the past five thousand years. In this century, youngsters seem to be maturing sexually at a younger age, and the problems of adolescence and the impact of cultural sophistication affect many of them by ages eleven or twelve. This fact has some bearing upon reading. Many educators and parents have thought of adolescence as a plateau, a time between childhood and adulthood when youngsters could pause to study and to learn. Some persons do seem able to delay adulthood even as they concentrate upon graduate school studies.

However, as I examine the disabled readers in the innercity high school, where I served as reading consultant for ten years, and compare them to the suburban students I now work with in a similar capacity, I find no happy plateau. Far from delaying adult emotions and involvements so they can concentrate upon school, the disabled adolescent reader's emotional and academic problems are inseparably mixed. In the innercity school, many disabled readers have out of wedlock babies, have hard drug problems, or may spend a great part of their time in courts and jails to such an extent that it seems futile to assume disabled readers will learn to read if one merely helps them attain some missing skills. Students also need help with overwhelming adolescent problems.

Perhaps the most important thing we can learn from research into adolescence is that each pupil is unique, with his or her peculiar patterns of potentiality and experience. Even physiologically students vary greatly and this has implications for reading. Some children are ready to read as young as ages four, five, or six. Girls seem to develop earlier than boys, and at adolescence there is a clear pattern of relationship between physiological development and learning. Children who mature physically at an early age tend to score higher on tests of mental ability. Boys who are larger and more mature develop more self-confidence as leaders and grow faster academically. Therefore, educators and parents need to take a second look at the underachiever in school in order to understand more fully why certain children do not appear to be developing to their full academic potential. In my work with hundreds of disabled adolescent readers, I have been left with one overwhelming impression: that self-image, the faith that one can succeed, is a need which transcends all others. These youngsters lack confidence in themselves. Many of them do not try to improve their reading because they are sure they will fail. I am reminded of what Erich Fromm says in *The Practice of Love* about how essential it is for one to have faith in himself, which means being willing to take a risk even if the result is failure. I am certain that the dependence which many of my pupils have upon drugs and alcohol is rooted in this lack of self-confidence.

It is essential for me, as a high school reading consultant, to deal with these emerging young adults as they are at the moment. I must know as much as possible about the emotions, needs, desires, and problems of each disabled adolescent reader, even though what has gone on before cannot be changed. The scars will always remain, but I can help students only as they learn to come with their wounds, as they build self-confidence for the future. If I must avoid assemblyline approaches and generalizations which never seem to apply to a specific case, then as I teach I must get well acquainted with specific young persons.

Sylvester

First, I want to tell you about Sylvester, who was born in an innercity black ghetto. He was number three of seven children, the second boy. He started to school at age five and one-half, and reports from his kindergarten and first grade teachers describe him as a quiet boy, willing to please, very small for his age. His first grade teacher indicated he was a slow learner and suggested he repeat first grade. However, such a large group of pupils entered the school the next fall that there was no room to keep him back, so Sylvester was placed in a "slower" second grade. In other words, at age six and one-half he was already marked for failure, was moved aside from the academic mainstream with consequences not only for his academic future but also for his adolescent self-esteem. No one seems to have asked whether Sylvester was small and docile for his age because of an inadequate diet. Nor did Sylvester's second and third grade teachers add any information to his record, except to give him C and D grades.

We do not know what Sylvester was feeling and thinking as he attended four different schools between first and fifth grades. We can be certain, however, that no one teacher knew Sylvester well enough to give him the positive support and encouragement he needed; for, by fourth grade, his record shows that he was rude, a discipline problem, had no study habits, and came to school physically unkempt. Being well dressed is psychologically crucial for the innercity child and perhaps for all children. Sylvester's fourth grade teacher did not recommend holding him back while he gained sufficient basic skills to keep up with his age level, nor is there evidence that anyone gave him special attention. By his fifth year of school, Sylvester had already been arrested twice for petty theft. Why did he steal? For clothing? For money? To bring something interesting into his unsuccessful life? In an effort to call attention to himself? Or was petty crime an area where he could demonstrate some skill, success, and accomplishment?

In these days, everyone is familiar enough with his sort of story to recognize that by the time Sylvester was in high school it was not enough to describe him as a disabled reader. He was, first of all, a disabled adolescent, a disabled person. Even if I devoted full time to him, how could I, as a reading consultant, help him read adequately unless I helped him at the same time to recover his sense of self-worth, to develop some hopes and goals in life that would motivate him to learn to read? Sylvester's reputation had preceded him to high school. He was not allowed to join the community boy's club because he was "belligerent and unmanageable." It appeared that no one had any faith in Sylvester, and he had no faith in himself. Perhaps some teachers were afraid to risk faith in him for fear he would not succeed and then they would have failed.

In the middle class suburb where I now work, I have no difficulty getting parents to come to see me to talk about how they can help their children. Indeed, I am sometimes pursued by mothers who want me to help improve the reading skills of sophomores or juniors who read on the fourteenth grade level—because mother wants her child's percentile rank increased from 90.8 to 99. But no teacher or counselor could enlist the cooperation of Sylvester's family in a plan to improve his academic skills or for anything else. His father left home when Sylvester was still in elementary school and no one knew where he was. Sylvester's mother worked long hours to try to support seven children, and she was too tired to come to school at night. She said she had no control over Sylvester anyway.

So what sense did it make to speak of Sylvester as an adolescent? He was an adult in that he had taken control of his own life. He was making his own decisions. He had fathered an illegitimate child. He was supporting himself, albeit illegally. Perhaps it was remarkable, now that Sylvester was sixteen, that he continued to come to school at all! Newspapers reported that in a similar city nearby, 40 percent of the innercity high school pupils are now dropping out in their junior and senior years. Why, from Sylvester's point of view, should he continue spending his time being sent out of first one class and then another? Twice, when she had been summoned to court, his mother asked the courts to "send him up" and to "get him out of her hair."

Late in his sophomore year (he was promoted along from year to year whether he had learned anything or not), the school psychologist tested Sylvester and found that although his potential seemed to be very low, he should not be classified as a special education student. So he was sent to the reading laboratory for help. Diagnostic tests showed what skills he needed, but how was he to be motivated? He was on drugs, was in and out of jail, and was drinking heavily. During the school day he slept most of the time, even in the reading class which he said he enjoyed. *He enjoyed reading class.* It was psychologically and emotionally rewarding to him to meet someone who cared about him, who gave him personal attention, who helped him establish some simple, achievable goals, and who gave him a sense of accomplishment in reaching them. In this context, it occurred to him that maybe he could get a job after all. It is important to note that he had long ago given up any such ambition, while nevertheless secretly aspiring to find a place in life like other people. So in the process of raising his reading skill by one grade level, he was taught to fill out a job application form correctly. It was suggested that he carry a copy of the form with him in case he needed to fill out an application some time. His progress reminds us how Paulo Freire found that illiterate adults can be quickly taught to read if they begin with words which are existentially meaningful to the individual. High school students who will not read basals such as *Dick and Jane* will show an interest in a driver's manual, a book on child care, an insurance policy, or even a basic course in elementary law.

I wish I could continue this happy side of Sylvester's story, but his problems outside of school and reading class were overwhelming. He got a job but lost it because he could not read the label on cans of paint. Shortly after that he knocked down an elderly man in a robbery attempt; the victim died, and Sylvester went to jail. Because of Sylvester's court case I was most interested to read in *Psychology Today* (*4*) the case of another boy in jail whose teacher went back to examine his school records to see where educators had failed him. That boy was much more talented than Sylvester; but the boy in the *Psychology Today* article had higher test scores and was, in a sense, the victim of a system which had immediately seized upon his reading deficiency as his only problem, as teachers sought to meet reading needs as discovered in diagnostic testing without examining a larger perspective of the boy's total need and emotional situation.

Blos (*1*) reports research which shows that young adolescents are becoming increasingly similar in lifestyle to older boys or girls, as the events which formerly took place in middle or adolescence seem increasingly to happen at younger ages. Sylvester's identity formation, personality consolidation, and character formation did not wait until his late teens or early twenties. To define him as a disabled adolescent suggests seeing how such formation happened early, perhaps too soon, leaving him an inadequate, disorganized, irresponsible person. On the other hand, parents and teachers may expect young people to act more adult than they are ready to be, expecting more of them than the teenagers are able to accomplish. The reverse may be equally true. Adolescents who are treated as children rebel, demanding to be recognized as emerging adults. In the case of Sylvester we see that he was thrust too soon into an adult world while at the same time being unable to accomplish (for example, read paint labels) on the level of the other adolescents at school. In these conflicts in the developing personality he was neither able to control himself nor could anyone else control him. He was both a child and an adult but was rarely an adolescent.

If we see adolescence as a time of maturing, a state of becoming as well as being, then it is clear that society failed to give Sylvester an adolescence, just as it failed to teach him to read. By the time he was in high school the two facts were inescapably intertwined. The innercity school recognized this fact in selecting realistic materials for pupils to read, thus giving these youngsters strong meat to chew which would have been censored and forbidden to them in another time and place. Since Sylvester daily confronted raw life on the street, there was no point in trying to shelter him at school.

Sylvester's mother and teachers tended to think of him as a rebel, in a time when many adults see adolescents in rebellion against authority. They complain: "He won't listen." "He won't cut his hair." "He will run away if I try to punish him." "He's useless and undependable." "Grades go down; he won't study; he is irresponsible." "It wasn't like that," they say, "when I was young." But where in Sylvester's file is there evidence that anyone ever saw things from his point of view? Fearful, insecure, lonely, powerless, restless, wounded, loosened from his moorings if he ever had any, Sylvester—typical of a high percentage of today's disabled readers—was wounded too young to have an adolescence, to define his own personality, to establish his own identity and goals. Somehow Sylvester passed from childhood into adulthood without knowing anyone who had confidence in him; without a sense of worth; without achieving faith in himself, in others, or in society.

Yet I remember that Sylvester made a bowl in woodworking class and, after he left school, the bowl was displayed in the hall case with other objects made by students during the next term. It was so lovely that teachers asked who had made it. I'm sure it was not deliberate, withholding the exhibition of his handcraft until after he was no longer in school; but what effect might this public showing have had on Sylvester if he could have heard some of the praise while he was still struggling with school? Still, how could reading be important from his point of view? He would readily admit that unless he learned to read better he would be ill-equipped to function in the world, but what use had the world for him anyhow? Sylvester wasn't even a very good petty criminal. He always got caught.

Jose

Jose was born in Puerto Rico where he attended elementary school through the fifth grade. His mother then sent him to Connecticut to live with his father because she had heard that the schools were much better in the states. As the eldest son, Jose was expected to lead the way for his younger brothers and sisters and to improve their family situation in the world. So Jose came with motivation and ambition, but it was difficult for a ten year old to fit into the new environment. Although Spanish was spoken at home, he used only English at school. It took him quite a while to make friends and to adjust himself to the new situation. Unlike Sylvester, Jose gave his teachers no problems. He was hard working and well behaved, so he was allowed to drift from grade to grade with his underachievement excused on the grounds that "He doesn't speak English."

When he entered high school, he was finally placed in English as a second language class (even though he did not qualify) since he had been in Connecticut for four years. Even so, Jose failed to get the attention he needed. He was so polite, well-dressed, was such a "really nice kid" that teachers overlooked his failure to accomplish. They failed the pupils who were serious discipline problems and rewarded Jose with a passing grade because he was so well behaved. In his junior year Jose organized a musical group for which he played the drums. A stinging experience for him occurred when he was offered a contract for a performance by the group and he could not read it. He realized that he had to learn to read, so in his senior year he was assigned to the lowest reading laboratory in the high school—one for high school pupils reading below the fourth grade level (3).

In the reading laboratory he became a different person, a delight to have in class, but also a student who recovered his motivation, lost his swagger, and developed a more mature self-confidence. He worked so hard in the laboratory that within four months he gained over two years on reading test scores. By March he had passed the fourth grade level and should have been moved up into the next lab, but because of his rapport with the reading consultant he remained in a room where she could provide him with an advanced individualized program tailored to his own needs. Perhaps the greatest moment came when his comprehension dramatically increased with the discovery that he could visualize the material he was reading. Never before had he been able to see "with his mind's eye" the picture which was being painted by the description. After that, his vocabulary and comprehension developed with speed.

On the surface, this success demonstrated the worth and methods of the reading laboratory. A boy who could hardly read at all was able to leave high school with adequate skills. But beneath the surface there is more to Jose's story. In spite of his earlier experience, he was able to develop self-confidence and a strong sense of who he was and where he wanted to go.

The problems of Jose and Sylvester were intensified by the student overload the teachers had and by the insensitivity of a system which sought to move students more or less automatically through an assembly line program which was the same for all pupils. Jose and Sylvester needed individualized, tailor made programs. No matter how much one tends to blame the teachers or the educational system, it is apparent that these boys brought adolescent problems into the high school which were only partly academic. They needed reading skills, but these skills could not be learned or were almost inaccessable because of other aspects of adolescence. Reading is still terribly important in our society, yet Jose—who as a junior in high school could not read his contract—might easily have been allowed to graduate without being able to read his diploma. He might have become increasingly bitter and hostile toward society for letting him graduate without skills to hold a good job. Certainly, this is what happened to Sylvester. By the time he was in junior high school, Sylvester realized that the schools were failing him whether he was failing school or not.

Those of us who teach and love our work and our students can understand how these tragedies can happen. No one teacher with a full load can possibly have time to investigate thoroughly the backgrounds of all students to get complete views of their problems and needs. Counselors, too, who may have a work load of three to four hundred students, do an overwhelmingly good job on the whole. Therefore, communities must take a close second look at the expectations they have of educational systems when they realize that the problems of Jose and Sylvester are not unique.

Anna Maria

The third case I want to report comes from a far different environment. Anna Maria lived in the suburbs and attended an excellent elementary school. Her parents were both professionals who tried to do all the right things—in contrast to the parents of Jose and Sylvester who had no books, magazines, or even newspapers in their homes. Anna Maria was the youngest of four children and grew up in a family which had camped and traveled together, played together, and read aloud together. Anna Maria's elementary school records do not reveal many perceptive or helpful remarks by her teachers who simply reported: "Anna Maria could do better work." or "Anna Maria should try more." When the parents visited the school, her teachers were enthusiastic with positive comments. Parents were not aided in seeing or understanding problems which were emerging.

Anna Maria's junior high school friends were from families whose interests were largely social and whose ambitions were limited. They were interested only in dating and in getting married as soon as they were out of high school, and Anna Maria's school environment was one in which pupils poked fun at those who were interested in reading or college. In order to fit in socially with her friends, Anna Maria quit using "large words" and hid the fact that she liked some of her subjects and teachers. She went along with her friends who were looking for fun and kicks through drugs, sex escapades, and shoplifting games—and knowing her family disapproved made her a rebel and alien at home. She sometimes stayed out until four o'clock in the morning on school nights and threatened to run away if her parents disciplined her. She cut school more and more until by January she was virtually a dropout. Part of Anna Maria's real difficulty resulted from the fact that parents and school kept comparing her to her older brothers and sister who had outstanding academic records. Teachers who should have known better often called her in to compare her poor school record with that of her siblings, which drove her further away from home and school. She decided she could never perform on the level of her brothers and sister and, therefore, was not interested in school at all. Her ambition was merely to quit school and get a job, which she did before she was sixteen. Her family could compel her to go back to school but could not compel her to learn or to succeed; by tenth grade, her reading scores had actually retrogressed until she found it difficult to read and write, even though she had read above level in fifth grade.

Put her in a reading laboratory? "Ridiculous," said school administrators. They could point to her high IQ scores, her family background, her demonstrated ability to perform in grade school. Her problem, they said, was a matter of discipline—drugs. In a sense this was true, but it was also true that she was using drugs to run away from an adolescence with which she could not cope. Other pupils might have a drug problem because they couldn't read, but surely Anna Maria had a reading problem because she was on drugs. She was placed in a drug dependence program where, as a result of personal attention, counseling, and a new sense of self-worth, she was able to solve her drug problem. But even afterwards (once she emerged from her drug stupor) she was a disabled adolescent reader because of falling behind during her many months on drugs. Again her case shows how many adolescents must solve a wide range of personal, emotional, and familial problems before reading problems are solved.

Summary

Now let me summarize some of my learning from these case studies. First, these cases reaffirm the complexity of adolescence and the variety of adolescent types. The need for an individualized program for each adolescent student is indicated; more important, the need for a much more comprehensive view of the needs and difficulties of each student is suggested. I want to express a fervent belief that more teachers must ask for and make use of information which is already available. I recognize the frustration of conscientious, caring, well-trained teachers who are staggered by the impossible load of teaching, corridor and lavatory supervision, counseling, and preparation which today's excellent teachers are expected to accomplish.

Often, however, when a teacher comes to me as a reading consultant to ask help with a particular student, I find the teacher has not yet looked at the student's personal file and has formed impressions about the student on the basis of gossip from other teachers and from superficial clues rather than tested fact. Teachers sometimes tell me that the records are there only for the use of counselors! I do not want to overlook the danger (which does exist) that an instructor will be negatively affected by a previous teacher's comments about a particular student. But how can we deal with complex adolescent problems, when many of us see a pupil only a semester or two for one period a day, if we do not trust one another's integrity and work together as a team? Competent teachers can certainly evaluate the remarks of other teachers, discriminating between prejudicial opinions and test score results.

The reading teacher must know much more than test scores. If a teacher knows, for example, that Dan is the sole support of his family and works at a job from 8:00 p.m. until 4:00 a.m., that teacher is more likely to be understanding and sympathetic—rather than sarcastic—when poor Dan falls asleep in the remedial reading laboratory. Yet I find that many teachers fail to inform themselves of such matters that do not require research to discover. The *Psychology Today* case of a young man who committed suicide while in jail for a crime he did not commit illustrates the complexity of the problems of the disabled adolescent reader. His family, school, and society refused to accept responsibility for various aspects in his development. The schools, of course, cannot be blamed entirely for his suicide; but, as the case unfolds through school records, it is evident the school failed to have a complete and comprehensive view of his needs and was content with totally inadequate proposals for solving his problems. Those of us who see the interrelationships between reading disability and other adolescent problems, those of us who are concerned and care about our students as whole persons, have a responsibility to help other teachers to become more involved in the development of each adolescent.

Teamwork is needed not only among teachers in dealing with the disabled adolescent, but also a larger teamwork is needed with other persons who have supplementary information and skills: physicians, psychologists, neurologists, oculists, speech and hearing specialists, social workers, attorneys, as well as reading specialists. The point of view and information of all such professionals must be brought together, even as early as kindergarten, for the pupil who appears to have problems. Such professionals should develop a comprehensive report, with information and treatment plans, as soon as a youngster is found to be in trouble. This is done promptly if a pupil is found to have leukemia; but if he is emotionally disabled or has fallen into delinquency or is lagging behind his peers in academic achievement such as in reading, a few Band-Aids are too frequently the only applications.

Our teamwork becomes just a pooling of ignorance and confusion unless it is grounded in better information about specific pupils. The one well thought of tracking system, for example, can be a horrendous cause of reading disability if it locks a pupil into a rigid mold without taking into account the fact that a poor reader may be an excellent mathematician, an outstanding artist, or a talented mechanic. In many ways, the most devastating fact about each of the three pupils whose cases I have cited is that their files revealed almost no information about their talents and abilities. There were negative comments like "no use suggesting college" or "a near hopeless case." But nothing was even reported about the modest goals of Sylvester or Jose. Did no one note that Sylvester could make a beautiful wooden bowl? Evidently not. Did no one discover that Anna Maria was astonishingly gifted at music? No, not even her family. In both innercity and suburban schools, teachers regularly received lists of students who were taking educational trips—playing in the band, singing in the chorus, visiting art museums—but seldom, if ever, were the names of remedial readers on the lists of these students who were receiving such extra fringe benefits. I cannot be convinced that these disabled adolescents were never on these lists because they lacked talents or interests. No, their talents, along with other facts about their personal lives which affect their reading skills, have not been uncovered. And, tragically, too often they have not been considered "worth the trouble." Not encouraged to set constructive goals, they were encouraged only to fail as readers and as persons.

I'm not suggesting that there is an Einstein hidden in every Jose or Sylvester. More adequate perspectives on the adolescent as a person will enable teachers to value simple and realistic goals and ambitions. Girls who may never go to college, for example, who become pregnant during their high school years, can be highly motivated to improve reading skills when they are given materials about baby care and are taught how to make books for their babies so as to increase the reading ability and interests of their children. Certainly, whether one is a reading consultant, counselor, principal, or teacher, one must know when he/she has reached the limits of one's capacity to help in a particular situation. But what one learns about a student must be shared with others, so that the pupil who has special needs will not be abandoned, and everyone becomes accountable for what happens to a Jose, an Anna Maria, or a Sylvester. If the community has out of school agencies to whom a disabled adolescent can be referred, even while in school, the educational system must actively work in partnership with all who can share information and cooperate in helping solve pupil problems. If needed facilities in the community do not exist, educators have a responsibility to help develop them so that the disabled adolescent is not dropped into a great void upon leaving school.

I suppose what this means, essentially, is that we must never lose faith. Somewhere along the line everyone lost faith in Sylvester, so he lost faith in himself. At the root of most reading disabilities there is someone's loss of faith at one time or another. I feel very strongly that once teachers lose faith in their own abilities to help pupils, or see adolescents losing faith in themselves, the teachers must immediately get a team of persons to work with the problem or turn the pupils over to someone else who can help. Most disabled adolescents lack contact with adults who believe in them, like them, have faith in them, will help them discover possible goals, and will help them gain the sense of accomplishment and self-worth which comes from success in meeting those goals.

Although we must focus on reading disability, let's not lose sight of the complexities of adolescence which lie at the heart of the phrase "disabled adolescent reader." Adolescents are individuals with their unique talents, strengths, weaknesses, dislikes, emotions, problems, and objectives. In dealing with pupils, schools and society must have clearer and more comprehensive views of them, at once particular and supportive and which recognize individuals as persons who are trying to emerge with some self-esteem, some skills, and some successes in solving problems.

Perhaps what emerges from these case studies can be framed as a question: Who is the disabled adolescent reader? Sylvester was disabled by his environment; Jose, perhaps by the educational institution; and Anna Maria, perhaps by home and peers. But each of these disabled adolescent readers needed first of all to be treated as a person who had the potential to overcome disabilities and make a unique contribution to society. No one teacher with a full load can have time to investigate thoroughly the backgrounds of all students. The problems of Jose, Sylvester, and Anna Maria are not unique—less than 50 percent of learning disabilities are diagnosed early and properly (2). Communities and school systems must take a close second look at what is demanded of teachers and disabled students and, the moment learning problems are first diagnosed, use teams of specialists to provide support for both teachers and pupils in a time when the problems of adolescence are overwhelming.

Recommended Readings

Coleman, James S. *Youth: Transition to Adulthood.* Chicago: University of Chicago Press, 1974.
Douvan, Elizabeth, and J. Adelson. *The Adolescent Experience.* New York: Wiley, 1966.
Friedenberg, Edgar Z. *The Vanishing Adolescent.* Boston: Beacon Press, 1959.
Freire, Paulo. "The Adult Literacy Process as Cultural Action for Freedom," *Harvard Educational Review,* 40 (May 1970), 205.
Goodman, Paul. *Growing Up Absurd.* New York: Random House, 1956.
Gottleib, Donald (Ed.). *Youth in Contemporary Society.* Beverly Hills, California: Sage Publications, 1971.

Havighurst, R.J., et al. *Adolescent Character and Personality.* New York: Wiley, 1949.

Jennings, K.K., and R.G. Niemi. *The Political Character of Adolescence.* Princeton, New Jersey: Princeton University Press, 1974.

Kagan, Jerome, and Robert Coles (Eds.). *Twelve to Sixteen: Early Adolescence.* New York: W.W. Norton, 1972. (Same as *Daedalus* articles in references.)

Kandel, B., et al. *Youth in Two Worlds.* San Francisco: Jossey Bass, 1972.

Kiell, Norman. *The Adolescent through Fiction: A Psychological Approach.* New York: International Universities Press, 1959.

Maring, Gerald H. "Paulo Freire's Method of Teaching Beginning Reading," unpublished paper.

Rice, F. Philip. *The Adolescent.* Boston: Allyn and Bacon, 1975.

Report of the White House Conference on Youth, U.S. Government Printing Office, April 1971.

Whitlock, J.K. "Causes of Childhood Disorders: New Feelings," *Social Work,* 21 (March 1976).

References

1. Blos, Peter. "The Child Analyst Looks at the Young Adolescent," *Daedalus,* Fall 1971, 961.

2. Gaylin, Judy. "Helping Learning Disability Children," *Psychology Today,* April 1977.

3. Rossman, Jean. "How One High School Set Up a Reading Program for 500 Students," *Journal of Reading,* 20 (February 1977), 393.

4. Sullivan, Patricia. "Suicide By Mistake," *Psychology Today,* October 1976, 90.

5. Tanner, J.M. "Sequence, Tempo, and Individual Variation in the Growth and Development of Boys and Girls Aged Twelve to Sixteen," *Daedalus,* Fall 1971, 908.

Reading Disability and Family Dynamics

James J. Garrigan
Joseph P. Kender
Warren R. Heydenberk
Lehigh University

No one will deny that children are the sum total of their environment as well as their genes. As teachers, we realize that children in our classes are profoundly influenced by their families, and this influence is, perhaps, the single most overriding factor that affects their learning and behavior through their school years, and, indeed, their entire lives.

In particular, children who are socially and emotionally disturbed frequently present histories of serious family disruption. Disturbance in the interrelationships among members of the family creates a home environment which is characterized by uncertainty, insecurity, and stress for parents and children alike. This uncertainty and stress are often the precipitating causes of emotional and social problems that trigger and then help to perpetuate serious educational problems in some children. The family unit, then, may be viewed as a biosocial subsystem within a larger cultural-social system, of which the school is an integral part. Herein lies the link between the home and the school.

The child guidance movement and family therapists have recognized the need for greater family involvement in the treatment of children with emotional and behavioral problems. It is our conviction that healing in its most sacred sense takes place between those who are related and relating. Despite the fact that the school is in a unique position to move in the direction of providing help for the entire family, family counseling has been delegated to guidance clinics. The school in some ways is really in a better position to offer these services. For one thing, the disturbed child is present in the school, and school personnel can make observations firsthand. Teachers are often the first individuals to be aware of family difficulties because a child's behavior in school often acts as a barometer of family disturbance. Furthermore, while some parents are reluctant to consult mental health professionals, these parents tend to be more receptive to help from school personnel because the school is more familiar to them and more in tune with the family's experiential frame of reference. The school is viewed by many individuals as an extension of family functions of teaching, guiding, and valuing.

It was this line of reasoning that led Garrigan and Bambrick in 1973 to develop a program of family therapy in the Centennial School, a school for social and emotionally disturbed children operated by the School of Education of Lehigh University. The basis for the program was a model called the Go Between Process which had been developed by Zuk (5). Garrigan and Bambrick wanted to study the effects of the Go Between Process of family therapy with families of emotionally disturbed children enrolled in the Centennial School. The researchers were interested in finding answers to these questions: 1) Is it possible to teach, quickly and effectively, a specific theory and method of family therapy to school personnel, namely classroom teachers, reading specialists, counselors, administrators, and school psychologists? 2) Are school personnel able to apply effectively what they have learned? The answer to both questions to date is a qualified "yes." Answers to these questions (*1, 2, 3*) were obtained by means of a rigorous experimental design that included adequate controls and valid measures of relevant variables. The results of the investigation showed the following:

1. The children of treated families showed less disturbed behavior in the classroom than children of untreated families.
2. Treated families reported less disturbed behavior of their children at home.
3. Parents in treated families reported that they communicated better with one another.
4. More of the children from treated families returned to regular classrooms when compared with a group of children from untreated families.

The training program devised by Garrigan and Bambrick focused on a selected group of teachers, reading specialists, and administrators, as well as on counselors and school psychologists, and demonstrated that school personnel who have little background in family therapy can function in this role with some degree of effectiveness. This is not to say that these individuals have become sophisticated family therapists even after 150 hours of training. The success of the program, which has been replicated in four different yearly field studies, does indicate that school personnel have absorbed some basic techniques and have been able to apply these techniques effectively within a prescribed setting and in a prescribed number of interviews.

In 1976, an integrated project was devised between the Family Therapy Program and the Reading Clinic at Lehigh University. It was noted that many of the emotionally disturbed children had reading difficulties. As it is known, within the context of poor readers is the child whose reading difficulty is secondary to certain external influences. Among these influences are emotional factors. Rabinovitch (4) specifies some of these factors as "negativism, anxiety, depression, emotional blocking, and psychosis...." A case study approach was undertaken which became the basis for a symposium presented at the Twenty-Second Annual Convention of the International Reading Association held in Miami Beach. A case history and videotape presentations of an afflicted child, of his family undergoing therapy, and observations of Centennial School personnel were used to demonstrate the interlocking functions between the family system and reading difficulties and the link between reduction of tension within the family and an improved climate in which the child was able to function better.

In a more experimental vein, Garrigan and Heydenberk investigated the effects of family therapy on visual perception, word recognition, and reading and listening comprehension of emotionally disturbed boys who were clinically described as cases of secondary reading retardation. The results are being prepared for publication.

Further work is proceeding between the Family Therapy Program and the Reading Program at Lehigh. It is our belief that family therapy cannot be relegated to a chosen few therapists. We believe that educators can obtain a modicum of competence in bringing to bear family strengths upon educational issues. We are not predicting that increased awareness on the part of school personnel of family dynamics and the effect these dynamics have upon school learning will result in dramatic improvement in skill areas such as reading. We do feel, however, that the reduction of tension and anxiety in the family can result in the lessening of the effect of emotions that cause numbing anxiety, psychic disorientation, and cognitive confusion in children.

Reduction of anxiety symptoms in the family can allow children the opportunity to turn their perceptions outward toward the acquisition of skills such as those that enable them to read. We feel that school personnel have a vital part to play in resolution of family problems and their effect on the emotional and academic growth of children. While it may be optimistic to think that all teachers would be willing to be trained in the techniques of family therapy, certainly, some key school personnel (counselors, psychologists, school nurses, principals) should become aware of the possibilities such training would offer to them in dealing with parents and children who are consistently called to their attention by reason of recurrent emotional, disciplinary, and physical problems.

References
1. Garrigan, James J., and A. F. Bambrick. "Short Term Family Therapy with Emotionally Disturbed Children," *Journal of Marriage and Family Counseling*, 1 (1975), 379-385.
2. Garrigan, James J., and A. F. Bambrick. "Family Therapy for Disturbed Children: Some Experimental Results in Special Education," *Journal of Marriage and Family Counseling*, 3 (1977), 83-93.
3. Garrigan, James J., and A.F. Bambrick. "Introducing the Novice Therapist to Go between Techniques of Family Therapy," *Family Process*, 16 (1977), 237-246.
4. Rabinovitch, Ralph D. "Reading and Learning Disabilities," *American Handbook of Psychiatry*, Volume 1. New York: Basic Books, 1959.
5. Zuk, G. H. *Family Therapy: A Triadic Based Approach*. New York: Behavioral Publications, 1972.

Dyslexia: Deficit in Reading or Deficit in Research?

Renate Valtin
Paedagogische Hochschule
Berlin, West Germany

Overview of Research Studies

Despite over thirty years of research on specific reading and writing disabilities in children with normal intelligence, the results are contradictory as indicators of either causes of the disabilities or remedial programs that can help persons overcome them. In recent years, numerous empirical investigations have changed some of the earlier concepts about dyslexia: Instead of a single causal factor, a variety of possible preconditions are now being emphasized (Vernon, 1977); and dyslexia, which was once regarded as an "isolated" phenomenon, is revealing itself to be an ever broadening disturbance of learning capacity.

As the present author began her work on dyslexia, professionals held relatively clear opinions about the manifestations and causes of dyslexia (*6, 7, 31*). In general, the following hypotheses were proposed: 1) Dyslexia is related to disturbances in visual perception (for example, difficulties in the recognition and differentiation of figures); 2) a basic phenomenon of dyslexia is directional confusion, which was believed to show itself in reversal and rotation errors, especially while reading, and in rotation of figures and left/right confusion; 3) left-dominance (left-handedness, left-eyedness, and mixed eye-hand dominance) was postulated as a causative factor in dyslexia, in conjunction with disturbed spatial abilities; 4) dyslexia was believed to be a congenital

Adapted from *Reading Research Quarterly*, 14 (1979), 201-221.

(inborn) weakness and, therefore, relatively independent of the sociocultural milieu.

However, the results of the few empirical studies conducted in Germany were not consistent. Methodological weaknesses in the research should be considered as possible grounds for the discrepancies; one should examine 1) uncertainty in the diagnosis of dyslexia, insofar as this was not based on standardized measures; 2) variations in the line drawn between dyslexic children and those who were believed to be merely less academically talented in the areas of reading and writing; 3) limited samples which were also heterogeneous in respect to age, sex, and even degree of reading retardation; 4) biased selection of dyslexics, who were frequently clinical cases referred by school psychologists or a reading clinic (the cause of referral generally being not the dyslexia itself but secondary disturbances in behavior); 5) the absence of appropriate control groups; and 6) the lack of reliable and objective testing techniques.

In order to eliminate or at least to reduce some sources of error, the research of the present author tried several methods (*34, 36*).

1. The diagnosis of dyslexia was undertaken operationally by the use of standardized test procedures. The criteria were an IQ of 90 or more and a percentile rank of 5 or less on a standardized spelling test. In her later studies, Valtin (*35*) used a percentile rank score of 15 or less.

2. The children studied were selected from among regular school classes by means of tests.

3. Control groups were chosen so as to hold constant as many characteristics believed pertinent for dyslexia as possible. This was done by matching dyslexics with children of at least average spelling ability, so that the pairs were comparable in respect to age, sex, year in school, IQ, and father's profession. The possible failings in such matching procedures will be discussed later.

The first study (*34*) was based on 100 pairs of dyslexic and normal children and produced the following results:

1. For most of the dyslexics, failures in reading and writing were not connected with disturbances of visual perception. This was indicated by the *Benton Test* and by other visual tests. Thurstone's test of Perceptual Speed—subtest of the *Primary Mental Abilities* (PMA)—measures the ability to distinguish rapidly between like and unlike figures. Surprisingly, on it, the dyslexic children were actually faster than the nondyslexics. The unexpected superiority of dyslexics on this visual test has also been observed by Kemmler (*17*) and Machemer (*18*).

2. There were no indications of disturbed spatial abilities among the dyslexics; this finding was confirmed by factor analysis. The scores on the reading, perception, and spatial tests were separately intercorrelated for both groups. In each case, a factor analysis was carried out and the factorial structures of both groups were compared; the results were comparable, with only minor discrepancies. The results of the factor analysis, therefore, reinforced the results of the study of matched pairs.

3. Left-handedness, left-eyedness, and mixed eye-hand dominance—measured by the *Harris Tests of Lateral Dominance* and by the *A-B-C-Vision Test*—showed no relationship to dyslexia, to difficulties in spatial orientation, or to reversal and translocation of letters in reading and writing.

4. Although the samples had been matched for father's profession, interviews with the parents of dyslexics and of good spellers showed a large number of significant differences in respect to the sociocultural milieu of the children. Dyslexia was correlated with limited education of the mother, large number of children in the home, birth order, crowded living conditions, and lack of interest in reading on the part of the parents. Moreover, there were indications of backwardness in speech development and a greater frequency of speech disturbances among the dyslexics.

Since the design of this correlation study does not permit any conclusions as to the causes of dyslexia, further studies were used to investigate the hypothesis that intervening variables, such as particular personality characteristics and speech factors might underlie the correlations (*35, 36*). Once more the method of matched pairs was used. As predicted, the dyslexics showed lower motivation for achievement on a 1963 German version of the *Thematic Apperception Test* (TAT) revised by Meyer, Heckhausen, and Kemmler; higher anxiety levels and greater cognitive field dependence were indicated by an Embedded Figures Test. Since research in social psychology has revealed a connection between these specific personality characteristics and early training of the child for independence (*16*), a questionnaire like one used by Winterbottom (*42*) was used to elicit data on child rearing methods from the mothers. One should keep in mind the weaknesses of such an ex post facto study, in which primary and secondary (that is, reactive) personality characteristics can scarcely be separated. Yet the findings permit us to suggest cautiously that the limited motivation and field dependence of the dyslexic children may not be merely a reaction to the reading failures the child has experienced, but possibly may be in part a result of influences in early childhood training.

The dyslectic children of the Valtin sample showed significantly poorer results in tests of articulation and auditory discrimination. Other language abilities were assessed by a vocabulary test (WISC), a concept formation test (classification of pictures, used by Olver and Hornsby, 1967), and the *Verbal Expression Test* of the ITPA (Kirk, McCarthy, and Kirk, 1968). Only the vocabulary test yielded significant differences. A vocabulary subtest analysis confirmed the results reported by Belmont and Birch (*15*) that the dyslexics gave a larger percentage of descriptive and a lower percentage of categorial definitions. A further analysis of the oral speech of the dyslexic and the normal children failed to reveal significant differences in the grammatical structure of oral language.

In view of the significantly poorer achievement of the dyslexics in an oral arithmetic test, these data suggest that, in the case of many of these children, dyslexia is only one aspect of a broader learning disability, which is frequently coupled with auditory and speech-motor deficiencies and specific personality characteristics (anxiety, failure motivation, and cognitive field dependence).

Later German research studies which also used the matched pair design were essentially in agreement with the above presented results (*9, 2, 22, 23*).

A Critique of Various Approaches to Dyslexia

It seems useful at this point to identify the different approaches which try to assess the problem of dyslexia and to analyse their implicit assumptions and inherent difficulties. The above cited research studies of the present author are an example of the etiological and the deficit approach which, in a retrospective view, seem inadequate to assess dyslexia.

The Etiological Approach

The etiological approach tries to identify physical, environmental, and emotional factors which impede the reading and/or spelling process. There seem to be at least three inherent difficulties of this approach:

1. *Lack of criteria for differential diagnosis and the problem of overlap.* Rabinovitch (*25*), for example, categorizes reading problems into three major groupings: primary reading retardation, secondary reading retardation, and brain injury with reading retardation. But he admits very frankly that the criteria for differential diagnosis are still

uncertain and "Despite the neatness of all our attempted theoretical formulations, I must confess that in practice our group not infrequently arrives at a diagnosis such as 'a secondary retardation with a touch of primary disability'."

2. *Uncertainty of the direct causal relationship.* As the marvelous interdisciplinary study of Robinson (*27*) reveals, there was a lack of agreement among her group of specialists as to which factor caused the reading problem. There is no theoretical agreement whether these factors are causative, contributory, or merely coincidental to the reading retardation. We also lack practical evidence for a direct causal relationship. As Merritt (*20*:186) points out: "In the case of every factor that is supposed to contribute to reading disability, we can find a child who should be at risk who can read perfectly well."

The research should look for the missing link, the mechanisms in which way these causative or contributory factors may affect certain reading subskills, and we need a fruitful theory of the reading process as a precondition for this.

3. Another problem of this approach is the *low and indirect therapeutical value.* Having diagnosed etiological factors as brain damage or poor home conditions, the teacher is unable to remove or correct these factors. Furthermore, this approach does not give any direct evidence for specific remedial instruction as we do not know the operating mechanisms and the points in the reading process where these factors lead to a disturbance. As Merritt puts it: "If a child's difficulty with orientation does owe something to a neurological deficit of some kind, we certainly cannot operate on his brain. Whatever may have predisposed the child to experience difficulty, the remedial problem consists of developing the appropriate learning sets. This is where more attention is really needed both for practical and theoretical reasons."

The Deficit Approach

The deficit approach looks for deficits of dyslexic children in various cognitive functions. Again, there are many shortcomings of this attempt.

1. *The assumptions about the reading process underlying the deficit approach are inadequate.* It is significant that in studies of this type one scarcely ever finds a definition of the reading process that goes beyond banal paraphrases (reading is making sense out of signs), let alone a discussion or proposal of a theory of reading. Authors are content to list the skills used during reading and writing. Behind most of these research studies lies the unexpressed assumption that reading is

the sum of a variety of cognitive functions (such as visual and auditory discrimination, language skills, memory, and comprehension of symbols. It is implicitly assumed that the undisturbed functioning of these processes guarantees reading achievement and that reading will be impaired if one of these functions is deficient. That reading is a result of a specific learning and instruction process seems to be ignored in this model. Consequently, dyslexia most often implies a specific causal attribution: The causes are primarily attributed to the children and their lack of capacities and not so much to the instruction process itself.

Most of the research on dyslexia is based on this "function model": Groups of dyslexic children and normal readers are compared in these functions, and low achievement of backward readers is interpreted as a deficit which impedes normal progress in reading. The fallacy of this conclusion is obvious. Correlations are interpreted as causal factors, though the design of the studies does not permit this.

The function model also serves as a theoretical basis for the remedial treatment. The deficient visual, auditory, and motor functions are trained by specific programs and the improvement of these functions—so it is hoped—will result in an improvement of reading (see, for instance, the Frostig program). There is, however, neither theoretical nor empirical evidence for the validity of such a transfer, and the numerous American experiments with visual training programs have not proved themselves helpful in increasing reading achievement (38). In Eggert, et al.'s study (9), the motor and cognitive-verbal training (that is, training in writing and functional exercises) resulted in very unspecific effects: Both groups showed improvement in both the trained and the untrained areas.

Thus, the assumption of a transfer from those training programs is questionable. Moreover, when one looks at the low correlations which have to date been obtained between the functions which have been tested and the reading achievement scores, the impression arises that factors have been measured that are rather irrelevant to the reading process. A further verification for this is that, in a longitudinal study by Valtin (35), scarcely any relationships worth mentioning were observable between reading achievement in the first, second, and third school years and some variables measured at the beginning of school (visual perception, directional confusion, articulation, auditory discrimination, vocabulary, school readiness). Although the correlations between these variables and reading achievement were statistically significant, they were of no great practical value; for instance, individual predictions of reading failure were not possible.

2. Another objection against this approach is the circumstance that the observed *deficits of the poor readers might be an artifact of the research method used.* If we compare representative samples of good and poor readers, they will differ in background variables such as intelligence and socioeconomic status and, consequently, they will differ in correlated psychological tests of visual, auditory, memory, or language abilities. Thus the poor readers will show many "cognitive deficits." But if we take into consideration the IQ of the poor readers and investigate only children with specific reading disabilities—individuals whose reading progress is unsatisfactory in terms of their potential—then the deficits will vary with the measure of potential ability we use (Verbal IQ, Performance IQ, or Full Scale IQ).

As Reed (*26*) and Valtin (*39*) have demonstrated, the IQ measures used to define the reading disability not only influence the pattern of the relationship between Verbal and Performance IQs but also the results in tests correlating with these IQ measures. If groups of dyslexic and nondyslexic children were matched on Performance IQ, the poor readers showed deficits especially in the language tests. If the Verbal IQ was chosen for the matching, the differences tended to disappear. When the Full Scale IQ was used as the matching variable, the poor readers showed better results in the visual tests and poorer results in the language tests.

Other studies using the matched pair design also showed a superiority in the visual domain (*23, 17, 34*). In the Valtin (*39*) study, the results even varied in those variables which are frequently quoted as reliable deficits of reading disabled children, such as poor vocabulary, field dependence, poor auditory discrimination abilities, memory for digits, coding, and symbol learning. These results support the hypothesis of Reed (*26*) that deficits of poor readers are artifacts of the matched pair design and our definition of dyslexia.

To explain these results, Reed turns to the principle of the correlation between two and more variables. When matching is done on the basis of Verbal IQ, good and poor readers will show similar scores in those variables which correlate higher with Verbal IQ than with reading achievement. They are more likely to be different in characteristics that are more closely related to reading achievement than to Verbal IQ. When on the other hand the Performance IQs of both groups are comparable, good and poor readers will achieve similar scores in tests that are highly correlated to Performance IQ. Thus, conclusions about lower achievement or deficits among children with specific reading difficulties on cognitive, speech, or visual tests can only be drawn with extreme care.

In summary, we can state that the acceptance of the etiological approach and the deficit approach has had two unfortunate consequences:

1. It has led researchers in a circle round about the reading process (in areas such as sociocultural milieu, dominance factors, early childhood development, personality characteristics) while we scarcely know anything about specific deficits in the reading process itself.

2. Since the method of matched pairs was chosen for data collection, the results—in respect to the recorded deficits—are not reliable and are possibly artifacts of the research design and the IQ measure used to define specific reading disability.

The Process Oriented Approach

A fruitful alternative to the function model is the *process oriented approach*, which tries to identify partial processes of reading in which dyslexic children are deficient (*40, 28, 29, 30*). German psychologist Scheerer-Neumann has outlined a model of reading limited to the reading of single words, a process which has been influenced also by American researchers such as Mackworth and Gibson (*10*). According to this model, three operations take place sequentially during the process of word identification:

- The visual operation consisting of a distinctive feature analysis and a segmentation of the visual materials into chunks,
- the phonetic recoding, and
- the semantic decoding.

Scheerer-Neumann's studies (*28, 29, 30*) show that dyslexics have difficulties with the segmentation of words into economical units because they either try to read words as a whole (guessing) or try to recode letter by letter. In a tachistoscopic experiment, the performance of good and poor readers in identifying eight item pseudowords of either first or fourth order approximation to German were compared (*aejnaite* and *pulmerat*). Both groups showed better results with the more redundant pseudowords, but the difference between these two experimental conditions was much greater for the dyslexics, who apparently could not profit from the better segmentation possibility of the fourth order pseudowords. Another experiment showed that the identification of pseudowords by poor readers could be improved when the stimulus material was segmented into syllables (*29*).

Still another study of Scheerer-Neumann throws an interesting light on the reversal errors of poor readers which, within the *deficit approach*, are linked to a directional confusion. Using letter sequences ordered by chance, the poor readers were even better than the good ones in reporting the left-right sequence; but the good readers showed better results when letter sequences were used which could be segmented into chunks. Thus, it is apparent that the poor readers have internalized the left-right scanning process but fail because of their "uneconomical segmentation strategy": If the phonetic coding process operates on syllables (*pul-me-rat*), the order of the letters within the syllable is already fixed; but if one recodes letter-by-letter *p-u-l-m-e-r-a-t*), it is far more difficult to keep the right order (*30*).

As Scheerer-Neumann (*28*:134) points out, her reading model has to be refined, inasmuch as the mastery of the partial processes must be investigated under three aspects:

- The degree to which these operations are developed,
- the speed of the processes, and
- the degree to which these operations have become automatic.

Interfacilitation among these processes is another aspect worthy of study. Furthermore, this model must be elaborated for reading passages (words in context) where other language and cognitive skills are involved. Some comprehension difficulties of poor readers have been analyzed by Golinkoff (*11*).

Goodman's miscue analysis may also give evidence about individual variations in reading processes and about the kind of information (graphic-phonetic, syntactic, or semantic) dyslexic children process in interacting with a given text. A pilot study by Hofer (*15*) has identified individual differences in the reading strategies of dyslexics.

- Difficulties in word identification: Children are so busy recoding letter by letter that they do not get the meaning,
- difficulties in the segmentation of the words in economical and meaningful units, and
- difficulties in using syntactic and semantic restrictions of the text.

We need further studies of this kind to identify the individual difficulties in the reading process and their interaction. Only those research studies that clarify individual components of the reading process, itself, can provide the practitioner with concrete guidance in the structuring of classwork.

The Subskill or Task Analysis Approach

Another promising approach to assess specific difficulties of dyslexia may be labeled the *subskill* or *task analysis approach*. Guthrie *(13)* and Guthrie and Seifert *(14)* identify subskills or direct components of the reading process with respect to the development of phoneme-grapheme association skills.

Guthrie found that the strengths in subskills in the group of poor readers were similar to those of the comparable subskills in normal readers with a similar reading level but were inferior to those of normal readers of the same age who completely mastered these skills. While the intercorrelations among the subskills were high positive for the normal readers, they were largely insignificant for the poor readers. Guthrie suggest that "Interfacilitation among subskills is necessary for normal reading. One source of disability for poor readers is lack of integration and interfacilitation among subskills."

Guthrie and Seifert, in a longitudinal study, demonstrated that the acquisition of letter-sound-correspondence rules was similar for good and poor readers and depended on the complexity of the rules. The specific tasks (including consonant vowel combinations, short vowel words, long vowel words, special rule words, and nonsense words) formed a hierarchy of difficulty and might be used for diagnostic and remedial purposes because they reveal specific strengths and weaknesses of the poor readers in word identification.

A Criticism of the Concept of Dyslexia

While it is generally agreed that dyslexia is due to multiple causation, there is considerable disagreement as to which factors are more relevant and which remedial procedures are more promising. There seem to be at least two reasons for these discrepancies: The variety of different approaches which try to assess dyslexia and the concept of dyslexia itself. This concept is a purely formal one and each researcher can more or less arbitrarily choose the operational definition and the criteria concerning the degree of reading retardation and the measure of intelligence. In Germany this issue becomes even more complicated by the fact that most of the researchers use spelling tests or, in some instances, a combination of reading and spelling tests as a diagnostic tool for dyslexia ("Legasthenie"). The purely conventional character of the concept of dyslexia has been expressed most clearly by Angermaier (*3*:148).

Thus the concept of reading disability points to the multiple causal factors of a relatively limited learning disturbance: The higher one sets the percentage of dyslexics, the less limited the learning disability will be. And this percentage must be *set*: The limits of dyslexia have to be *determined, established,* not *recognized* or *discovered.* There is no unmistakable collection of symptoms or argument for a specific reading disability... the concept does not refer to an "illness" but, at most, to divergences toward the lower end of a continuum of performance that displays heterogenous composition and whose extent must be determined.

Also, if we look at the origins of the reading-spelling difficulties of so-called dyslexic children, we find the greatest possible variations of genesis. Thus, the concept of dyslexia is purely descriptive and by no means an explanation for these difficulties, although current usage assumes a causality ("This child reads poorly because s/he is dyslexic").

Despite the criticism presented here of the purely formal concept of dyslexia and the inadequate traditional approaches to dyslexia—i.e., the etiological and the deficit approach—the work that has been done up to now on dyslexia should not be thrown out wholesale. Dyslexia was a "useful invention" (*4*). It has contributed to the isolation of specific factors which do hinder reading and writing. There have also been encouraging results for educational practice. What years of well founded, scientific criticism of the school marking system in West Germany were not able to accomplish has now been achieved in several of the federal states because of the results obtained from research on dyslexics, namely, a breach in the wall of the traditional grading system. In order to spare poor readers the repeated frustration of bad grades, these children can now be relieved from receiving grades and from participation in classroom dictations. In addition, they are now entitled to remedial work in small groups (although in several of the federal states they must first present a "dyslexic's passport," so that the school observes its commission to transmit to all children the techniques of our culture even when this requires special remedial efforts). Precisely because dyslexia is not an illness, we must now demand that these privileges be extended not only to children with reading problems but to all children with weaknesses in any subject area.

References

1. Anastasi, Anne. *Differential Psychology: Individual and Group Differences in Behavior.* New York: Macmillan, 1966.
2. Angermaier, Michael. *Sprache und Konzentration bei Legasthenikern.* Göttingen: Hogrefe, 1974.

3. Angermaier, Michael. "Das neue Verständnis der Legasthenie und seine Auswirkungen," *Fernstudienlehrgang Legasthenie*, 5 (1974), 131-148. Weinheim: Beltz.
4. Angermaier, Michael. "Uber die Nützlichkeit der Erfindung der Legasthenie," *Bildvng und Erziehung*, 38 (1974), 300-306.
5. Belmont, Lillia ι, and Herbert G. Birch. "The Intellectual Profile of Retarded Readers," *Perceptual and Motor Skills,* 22 (1966), 787-816.
6. Biglmaier, Franz. *Lesestörungen. Diagnose und Behandlung.* München, Basel: Reinhardt, 1964.
7. Bleidick, Ulrich. *Lesen und Lesenlernen unter erschwerten Bedingungen.* Essen: Schneider, 1966.
8. Dykstra, Robert. "Auditory Discrimination Abilities and Beginning Reading Achievement," *Reading Research Quarterly*, 1 (Spring 1966), 5-34.
9. Eggert, Dieter, Karl D. Schuck, and Axel J. Wieland. "Ergebnisse eines Untersuchungsprogramms zur kontrollierten Behandlung lese-rechtschreibschwache Schuler," in Renate Valtin (Ed.), *Einführung in die Legasthenieforschung.* Weinheim: Beltz, 1973, 140-155, 265-290.
10. Geyer, John J. "Comprehensive and Partial Models Related to the Reading Process," in Frederick B. Davis (Ed.), *The Literature of Research in Reading with Emphasis on Models.* New Jersey: State University of New Brunswick, 1971, 5-51.
11. Golinkoff, Roberta Michnick. "A Comparison of Reading Comprehension Processes in Good and Poor Comprehenders," *Reading Research Quarterly*, 11 (1975-1976), 623-659.
12. Goodman, Kenneth. "Reading: A Psycholinguistic Guessing Game," *Journal of the Reading Specialist*, 6 (1967), 126-135.
13. Guthrie, John T. "Models on Reading and Reading Disability," *Journal of Educational Psychology*, 65 (1973), 9-18.
14. Guthrie, John T., and Mary Seifert. "Letter-Sound Complexity in Learning to Identify Words," *Journal of Educational Psychology*, 69 (1977), 686-696.
15. Hofer, Adolf. "Lesediagnosen in der Grundschule mit Hilfe des Verlesungskonzepts," in Gudrun Spitta (Ed.), *Legasthenie gibt est nicht ... Was nun?* Kronberg: Scriptor, 1977, 38-50.
16. Kagan, Jerome, and Nathan Kogan. "Individuality and Cognitive Performance," in Paul H. Mussen (Ed.), *Carmichael's Manual of Child Psychology*, Volume 1. New York: J. Wiley and Sons, 1970, 1273-1365.
17. Kemmler, Lilly. *Erfolg und Versagen in der Grundschule.* Göttingen: Hogrefe, 1967.
18. Machemer, Peter. "Auslese und verhaltenstherapeutische Behandlung von Legasthenikern," in Renate Valtin (Ed.), *Einführung in die Legasthenie-forschung.* Weinheim: Beltz, 1973, 238-249.
19. Malmquist, Eve. "Factors Related to Reading Disabilities in the First Grade of Elementary School," doctoral dissertation, University of Uppsala, 1958.
20. Merritt, John E. "Reading Failure: A Reexamination," in J.F. Reid (Ed.), *Reading: Problems and Practices.* London: Ward Lock Educational, 1972, 186-195.
21. Neisser, Ulrich. *Cognitive Psychology.* New York: Appleton-Century-Crofts, 1967.

22. Niemeyer, Wilhelm. *Legasthenie und Milieu.* Hannover: Schroedel, 1974.
23. Oehrle, Brigitte. *Visuelle Wahrnehmung und Legasthenie.* Weinheim: Beltz, 1975.
24. Olver, Rose R., and Joan Rigney Hornsby. "On Equivalence," in Jerome S. Bruner, et al. (Eds.), *Studies in Cognitive Growth.* New York: Wiley, 1967, 68-85.
25. Rabinovitch, Ralph D. "Dyslexia: Psychiatric Considerations," in John Money (Ed.), *Reading Disability. Progress and Research Needs in Dyslexia.* Baltimore: Johns Hopkins, 1962, 73-80.
26. Reed, James C. "The Deficits of Retarded Readers: Fact or Artifact?" *Reading Teacher,* 23 (1970), 347-352, 393.
27. Robinson, Helen M. "Why Pupils Fail in Reading," *A Study of Causes and Remedial Treatment.* Chicago: 1946.
28. Scheerer-Neumann, Gerheid. "Funktionsanalyse des Lesens," *Psychologie in Erziehung und Unterricht,* 24 (1977), 125-135.
29. Scheerer-Neumann, Gerheid. "Prozeßanalyse von Lesestörungen," in Volker Ebel (Ed.), *Legasthenie.* Koblenz: Bundesverband Legasthenie, 1977, 63-83.
30. Scheerer-Neumann, Gerheid. "Die Ausnutzung der sprachlichen Redundanz bei leseschwachen Kindern: I Nachweis des spezifischen Defizits," *Zeitschrift für Entwicklungspsychologie und Pädagogische Psychologie,* 10 (1978), 35-48.
31. Schenk-Danzinger, Lotte. *Handbuch der Legasthenie im Kindesalter.* Weinheim: Beltz, 1971.
32. Schlee, Jörg. *Legasthenieforschung am Ende?* Munchen: Urban and Schwarzenberg, 1976.
33. Skjelfjord, Vebjørn. "Problems of Validity in Connection with the Concept of Auditory Discrimination between Speech Sounds," *Scandinavian Journal of Educational Research,* 19 (1975), 153-173.
34. Valtin, Renate. *Legasthenie - Theorien und Untersuchungen.* Weinheim: Beltz, 1970; Third Edition, 1974.
35. Valtin, Renate. *Empirische Untersuchungen zur Legasthenie.* Hannover: Schroedel, 1972.
36. Valtin, Renate. "Report of Research on Dyslexia in Children," paper presented at the annual convention of the International Reading Association, Denver, 1973. Eric Document Reproduction Service, 1973.
37. Valtin, Renate (Ed.). *Einführung in die Legasthenieforschung.* Weinheim: Beltz, 1973.
38. Valtin, Renate. "Grundsätze für die Betreuung legasthenischer Kinder," *Fernstudienlehrgang Legasthenie,* Volume 2. Weinheim: Beltz, 1974, 69-92.
39. Valtin, Renate. "Dyslexia: Deficit in Reading or Deficit in Research?" *Reading Research Quarterly,* 14 (1978-1979).
40. Vernon, Magdalen D. *Backwardness in Reading.* Cambridge: University Press, 1960.
41. Vernon, Magdalen D. "Varieties of Deficiencies in the Reading Process," *Harvard Educational Review,* 47 (1977), 396-410.

42. Winterbottom, Marion R. "The Relation of Need of Achievement to Learning Experiences in Independence and Mastery," in J. W. Atkinson (Ed.), *Motives in Fantasy, Action, and Society*. Princeton, New Jersey: 1958, 453-478.

Test References

A-B-C *Vision Test for Ocular Dominance.* Walter R. Miles. New York: The Psychological Corporation, 1953.

Benton Test (German revision). O. Spreen. Bern: Huber, 1961.

Harris Tests of Lateral Dominance. Albert J. Harris. New York: The Psychological Corporation, 1963.

Illinois Test of Psycholinguistic Abilities. Samuel E. Kirk, J. J. McCarthy, and W. D. Kirk. University of Illinois, 1968.

Primary Mental Abilities (German revision). Lilly Kemmler. *Erfolg und Versagen in der Grundschule.* Göttingen: Hogrefe, 1967.

Thematic Apperception Test (German revision). Wolf Meyer, Heinz Heckhausen, and Lilly Kemmler. "Validierungskorrelate der inhalsanalytisch erfaßten Leistungsmotivation guter und schwacher Schuler des 3. Schuljahres," *Psychologische Forschung*, 28 (1965), 301-328.

PART TWO

Aspects of Assessment and Planning for Instruction

Kindergarten Diagnosis and Training: A Program Report

Carroll Green
Rockwood School District
Eureka, Missouri

Carolyn Lyles
Woerther School
Ballwin, Missouri

Ann Eissfeldt
Ellisville School
Ellisville, Missouri

Educators have known for some time now that the only sure way to cure a reading disability is to prevent it from developing. Study after study tells us:

1. The earlier a reading disability is identified, the greater the improvement which follows.
2. The more severe the reading disability, the less chance there is that it can be totally and permanently overcome.
3. Many children who have a reading disability do not have a learning disability involvement. For some reason, they did not learn to read adequately through regular classroom instruction. These children are frequently noticed and provided remedial reading instruction at about third or fourth grade level when they are already a year or more below their reading expectancy levels. Unfortunately, they generally do not overcome this disability even though there is no clear explanation why they do not learn.

Many theories have evolved concerning the emotional involvements of children who, for several years, have felt they were failures in school because they could not read as well as their peers. Whether such damage to the self-concept does occur and whether it prevents later reading is still conjecture. It seems clear, however, that these children should have been able to read adequately from the beginning—if we could have identified their special needs and provided suitable training for them.

Rockwood School District decided to have their special reading teachers help primary teachers identify students earlier and try to evolve methods through which these students could learn. Our experience during the past three years has consistently supported the findings of other researchers. Those students who received special prereading training in first grade were far more successful than students who entered our district later and had not received help until third or fourth grade. However, these students still felt the discomfort of lagging behind their peers and the pressure of parents who frequently watched that first semester of first grade with fear and trembling lest Johnny might not be able to learn to read. Thus, we decided that if children's prereading development could be evaluated by mid year in kindergarten, it might be possible to develop the necessary skills at a time when such development is considered "normal." If this were possible, then these children should have a successful initial reading experience—avoiding any identification or label of reading disability or reading failure.

As we planned our strategies for teaching prereading skills to students in kindergarten, several important factors were considered. First, the skills with which we were concerned were, in most cases, already being taught in our kindergartens. Why were some children unable to develop these skills? Both research and our own observation told us that one critical factor was the child's ability to attend in a group situation. Some children appeared to be too distracted by other children and movement around them while others—though quiet and passive—simply did not seem to listen and participate enough to learn.

Second, little or no real diagnosis of specific skills was being done. As a result, students could not be directed to the specific kinds of activity which they needed most.

Third, there were few commercial materials available which provided suitable activities for the development of the specific skills needed. And, where commercial materials were available, it was generally assumed that the user would have considerable knowledge and skill concerning *how* the materials should be used. To solve these problems, we decided to

1. Diagnose student skill development. We used tasks selected from the Santa Clara Inventory of Developmental Tasks as well as some tasks we had developed ourselves. We checked only those skills for which we had planned direct instruction. The tasks involved the use of visual-motor skills, visual perception and memory, and language and conceptual development.
2. Provide individual tutoring for students with extensive skill deficits. This was achieved through the use of parent volunteers and student tutors.
3. Develop specific directives to guide the tutors in their work with students, and train the tutors in their use. Tutors were also trained to make the learning experience a success experience through programing the task, reinforcing the student's correct responses, and ending the session while the student is still enjoying it.
4. Develop teacher made activities where suitable commercial materials were not available.
5. Plan a record keeping system for the tutors which would indicate how the child is progressing in skill development and also how he/she feels about the work. Since tutors could not be observed at every session, this was a vital part of the plan.

Diagnosis and Tutoring

Our first big task was the diagnosis. The first year we tried just using teacher referrals and letting the counselor and special reading teacher do the testing. We limited the diagnosis and training to those few students that the teacher felt would probably have difficulty with reading. Testing confirmed that these children did have significant deficits on subtests of the Illinois Test of Psycholinguistic Abilities (ITPA).

During the second year of the program, we changed this procedure. Some children who should have had tutoring were overlooked—we wanted to locate and provide assistance for every child who needed it. Also, there were many children who had isolated skill gaps in their readiness development and the kindergarten teachers felt that it would be helpful to identify these needs. In order to screen all the students, we decided to use the assistance of parent volunteers. Each parent was trained to give one or two of the developmental tasks. The kindergarten teachers, the special reading teachers, the counselor, and the reading coordinator were also used to administer some of the tasks. The children rotated to each of the "stations" where the tasks were presented in a game format. Correct and incorrect responses were not indicated to the children so they did not feel the tension of a testing situation. The children were encouraged to feel pleased with their individual performances at each station.

These results were evaluated by the reading teacher. They were reported to the kindergarten teachers. The teachers planned large group activities to develop skills when it was found that many children needed such training. When only a few children needed more training, the skill was developed through small group instruction or learning centers, and for those with severe deficits, through the use of individual tutoring.

The teachers devised their own systems for keeping records of student progress. As tutors indicated that a child appeared to use a skill adequately, a teacher or an aide checked to be sure; then the child was moved to other activities. When a child did not appear to be making adequate progress, the reading teacher assisted in changing the activities and, with variations, continued work on the same skill or went to a different kind of task, letting the child return to the difficult skill later.

Parent Involvement

In addition to our work with students at school, we felt the need for support and involvement from the parents. We decided to develop this involvement through group meetings. The goals we had set up were

1. To reassure the parents that their child had not been singled out as a serious learning problem—we were not labeling children at all. If it seemed that there might be some more serious problem involved, then we would immediately recommend further testing and assistance from suitably trained specialists. Our goal was to help "normal" children have a successful initial reading experience.
2. To let parents know what kind of activities we would be using at school and to help them to understand the importance of such activities. For example, language development activities could be much more vital to the young children's preparation for reading than pencil-paper activities.
3. To suggest "fun" activities which parents could use at home to help prepare their children for successful reading experiences.

4. For parents as well as tutors, the importance of stressing the positive was emphasized. It is absolutely vital for children to believe in themselves and their capabilities. Mothers understand so well the feeling one has after preparing a delicious meal only to have someone say, "Your salad dressing is too sour today," and make no mention of the rest of the meal which took hours to prepare. Children feel much the same after laboring over their names, the alphabet, or their numerals only to be told, "But look, you have made your *b* backwards." Instead, we encouraged parents to remark, "I noticed you started your name with a capital letter and used lowercase for the rest. I'm really pleased with that." Those mothers who really want to know immediately that the dressing is too sour also may prefer to add, "Let me show you how to turn your *b* and, next time, every letter will be just right."

Parents were very responsive and seemed to appreciate the suggestions as well as the opportunities to share their concerns.

Results of the Program

During the first year, nineteen children received individual tutoring from parent volunteers or ninth grade student tutors. Five of these children now have moved out of our district, and one child was retained in kindergarten. That left thirteen children who entered first grade at our school. Our initial testing on the ITPA had shown improvement and the Metropolitan Reading Readiness tests were generally encouraging (see chart). Our real concern, however, was in whether these children actually succeeded in learning to read.

The last column on the chart shows the students' scores on the Gates-MacGinitie Reading Test, Form A-1, administered in April 1977 after seven months of reading instruction. We see that ten of the thirteen children have been successful. That is, 77 percent of those children whom kindergarten teachers identified as having significant skill deficits, and who might be expected to have difficulty in learning to read, were successful in their initial reading experience.

It was interesting to observe, while testing these children on the reading test, that every child had a very positive attitude toward reading. They did not simply mark answers at random. Although they did not complete the entire test due to time limits of the test, every item was read carefully and almost all of the responses they completed were correct. The children believed in their ability to read these items.

TEST RESULTS

Student	ITPA PRE	POST	Metropolitan* Readiness	Gates- MacGinitie
1	40	41	4	2.2
2	37	41	6	2.2
3	40	44	4	2.2
4	39	42	6	2.0
5	34	37	5	2.2
6	32	34	5	1.7
7	33	38	3	1.6
8	38	40	4	1.6
9	40	45	3	1.6
10	33	36	3	1.6
11	30	35	5	1.3
12	40	41	5	1.2
13	38	36	3	1.2

*Scale Scores are reported here.

We will continue to follow these children through third grade to see whether this initial success is maintained. More children have been tutored this year, but it is still too early to evaluate their success.

The program has certainly developed some positive results already, and parents and teachers are enthusiastic about this success. Teachers in other buildings as well as other parents have shown an interest in expanding the program into their own schools.

Summary

We are convinced that the following factors are critical to the success of this type of program:
1. Careful training and guidance of the tutors.
2. Maintaining a one-to-one ratio between tutors and children.
3. Diagnosing only those factors which appear to be directly related to reading and for which we have planned specific training activities.
4. Parent involvement throughout the program. This involvement must be positive and free from the fear that the child is handicapped or will be so labeled.
5. Stressing the importance of student success experiences—developing the "I can do it" feeling in each child.
6. Developing suitable materials which contain many manipulatives and are fun for children to use.

With these ingredients, your program could also develop the same kind of success story for those children who do not have learning disability handicaps—those who just need some individual attention to their specific needs.

Reading Diagnosis in the Classroom

Stella S. F. Liu
Wayne State University

In most school systems, reading diagnosis is done exclusively by diagnosticians and reading specialists rather than by teachers. Diagnosis usually is viewed as a specialized area requiring specialists with graduate degrees. Such persons often carry heavy caseloads, however, with the result that some students may go through a long waiting period before diagnosis. In such situations the teacher may, with training, be able to begin the diagnosis procedures in the classroom. Strang (*13*) introduced the concept of diagnostic teaching almost a decade ago. Her ideas about cooperation between teacher and specialist are relevant to many classroom situations today.

The teacher can begin diagnosis in some areas and skills to the limit that competence and time allow. Procedures which require specialized knowledge beyond the teacher's training can be done by the specialist.

This paper will present a diagnostic model for the assessment of reading skills and will discuss diagnostic strategies which teachers may be able to apply in the classroom. Reading problems which students may encounter fall into three general areas: cognitive, perceptual, and affective.

Figure 1 outlines these areas and specifies problems which fall into each component. This paper will deal with strategies for teacher diagnosis within one of the areas, the cognitive.

Cognitive assessment includes the following aspects: reading comprehension, the decoding process, word analysis skills, and intellectual abilities. The remainder of the paper is devoted to a detailed discussion of each aspect in the context of a classroom diagnosis of reading ability.

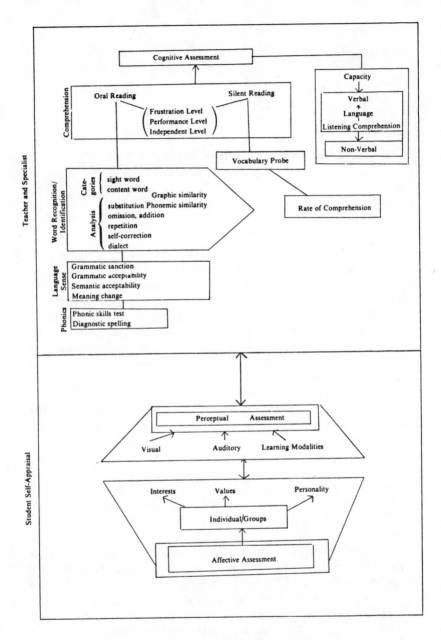

Figure 1. A Diagnostic Model

Liu

Reading Comprehension

The ultimate goal in reading is comprehension. Comprehension can be diagnosed from silent and oral reading with both formal and informal measures. The procedures described below can be applied by teachers in diagnosing from silent reading.

Standardized Tests

The single most commonly used measurement is the standardized achievement test. A number of states have mandated achievement testing at various grade levels (2, 3, 6, and 12 in California and 4 and 7 in Michigan, for example). Many school districts supplement state testing with additional testing for other grades. One purpose is the assessment of the standing of individual students in a class and assessment of average class performance against the established norm. Most often the teacher or a designated person administers the test. The test booklets are delivered immediately to the district central office, which in turn forwards them to the publisher for correcting. Neither teachers nor students see the booklets again, and test profiles often reach teachers months later—too late to be useful.

Standardized tests, however, can be used diagnostically, though teachers will want to use a test other than the one being used for state or district assessment purposes. The diagnostic use of standardized tests involves the following steps. This procedure is an adaptation of the vocabulary diagnostic probe developed by Rebecca Barr, which is discussed later in this paper.

First, after administering and scoring a test, give an unmarked copy of the test to the student. The teacher uses the student's marked test copy. Begin with the item above which five consecutive answers are correct and below which guessing is judged to have begun. Guessing is assumed to be taking place where one answer out of approximately every five is correct. Ask the student to read aloud the test item and answers and select the answer considered appropriate to him. The teacher should note any miscues the student makes on the marked test copy and indicate an *S* for the selected answer.

Second, if the answer is incorrect, the teacher simplifies the words for the student; the student again selects an answer, noted by *O* in the teacher's copy. This gives an indication about whether word recognition or identification causes problems in comprehension.

Third, if the answer is still incorrect, the teacher reads the item aloud to the student, thus providing further aid. This final selected answer is marked *L* for listening. The student then proceeds to the next item.

The same steps are repeated until five incorrect answers occur after the second step. This procedure helps to confirm that comprehension difficulties are not caused by word recognition and identification. The third step gives the teacher insight into the student's reasoning and strengths and weaknesses on comprehension.

In addition to this original score, the student has two more scores. One would be all the correct answers after the second step. This indicates that without word recognition and identification problems the student can comprehend at that level. The final score is an index of listening comprehension, ability to understand concepts, and relationships when material is read to the student.

Informal Measures

Included here are two procedures, the retelling of text and cloze procedures. Comprehension of text and other materials can be assessed by asking the student to retell what has been read and remembered. Criteria can be set up in advance, and retelling can be scored accordingly. If the student requires prompting with further questioning, a second score may be combined with the first to form a total score. Qualitative as well as quantitative indexes can be included in this measure.

Cloze procedure is another valuable method for assessing comprehension. Teachers can construct passages using cloze in different ways by deleting every tenth, fifth, or nth word or by deleting words of a specific category, such as nouns, action words, or adverbs. This procedure is described in Robert Bortnick, "The Case for Cloze in the Classroom," May 1974 [ED094327], among many other sources. Used diagnostically, this procedure tells the teacher how effectively the student uses context.

Diagnostic Probe on Vocabulary

Comprehension difficulty may arise from inadequate vocabulary, which can be diagnosed by using the vocabulary subtest in a standardized test. Barr (3) has developed a useful diagnostic technique for probing vocabulary. In her technique the teacher uses the marked test booklet of the student, and the student works from an unmarked copy of the test. The procedure consists of three sequential steps. First, the student reads the test item aloud and the teacher records any phonetic miscue. The student selects answers for the item, and the teacher marks *O* next to the oral response choice. Second, if the answer is incorrect, the teacher examines the student's word analysis skills and helps analyze words and their correct pronunciations. The student's responses are recorded. Third, if the answer is still incorrect, the teacher reads the item aloud to further determine whether the student can select the appropriate synonym. A notation of *L* for "listening" is placed next to the response choice. The probe stops if the student reads all the words included in the item independently for the first step, whether the correct response is selected. Upon completing the necessary probe of an item, the student proceeds to the next item. The same procedure is followed until the student has had difficulty with the first step on approximately five to seven consecutive items. The teacher should then discontinue the first two steps and continue to the end of the vocabulary section using only the third step.

The vocabulary probe should reveal whether weakness in word identification or in the language concept of word meanings causes problems in vocabulary development.

In contrast to silent reading, oral reading places extra demands on the reader and, thus, oral reading is not regarded as conducive to comprehension. Spache (*11*) has noted that in testing comprehension during oral reading, only the simplest questions of recall are possible. However, where silent and oral reading are similar processes in the first two primary years, oral reading comprehension may be assumed to be similar to silent comprehension. Even so, accuracy of oral reading does not reveal either silent or oral comprehension of the reader at any school level. Thus, oral reading is not recommended for testing for comprehension.

Decoding Process

While oral reading is not suitable for assessing comprehension, it is an excellent procedure for examining a student's decoding process (here decoding does not include comprehension). Such evaluations can involve use of standardized tests, informal diagnostic surveys, and miscue analysis.

A number of commercial tests include selections for oral reading which are intended to place a student at a reading level. The imperfect validity and reliability of the many tests critiqued by Spache make the value of such standardized tests questionable. However, the miscues generated from oral reading may be used for analysis of reading process.

Specialists have used the Informal Reading Inventory (IRI) since Betts (*4*) introduced it over thirty years ago. The three reading levels (independent level with 99 percent word recognition and 90 percent comprehension, instructional level with 95 percent word recognition and 75 percent comprehension, and frustration level with 90 percent word recognition and 50 percent comprehension) have usually been accepted. They have been challenged, however, by Nila Banton Smith, who suggested that these standards on word recognition and comprehension are too high. Powell (*9*) questioned the validity of the three levels assigned to a reader and agreed with Smith that the original criterion of 95 percent correct pronunciation for word recognition was too high. He also contended that the application of one set of performance standards uniformly across all grade levels was incorrect. He further argued that a reader does not have an instructional level because instruction is given by the teacher, and what a reader actually has is a performance level. For maximal learning, all three ingredients have to match: performance level of the student, instruction level provided by the teacher, and the appropriate difficulty of reading material.

An informal reading inventory is valuable because it evaluates strategies used by a reader in the reading process. Miscue analysis is one such procedure that affords the teacher the opportunity to examine in depth a student's reading behavior in the decoding process. The Goodman (*5*) and Goodman and Burke (*6*) miscue analysis procedure can be adapted for classroom use in abbreviated form. The oral reading of the student should be taped for analysis as follows.

On the word level, miscues are analyzed according to

1. Graphic similarity. To what extent is the response word similar to the text word, at the beginning, ending, or middle?
2. Sound similarity. To what extent does the response word sound like the text word, in the beginning, ending, or middle?
3. Grammatical function. Does the response word serve the same grammatical function as the text?

On the sentence level, miscues can be further analyzed by

4. Syntactic acceptability. Does the miscue make the sentence still syntactically acceptable?
5. Semantic acceptability. Does the miscue make the sentence semantically acceptable?
6. Meaning change. Does the miscue cause a change in meaning?

With this system, the teacher can analyze miscues of these common types:

1. Dialect and habitual association. The teacher should examine the student's miscues resulting from dialect influence and habitual association in which a name or key word is continually mispronounced. She/he should discount all dialect miscues and all but the first of habitual association miscues in the analysis.
2. Substitutions. This type is perhaps the most common miscue. Substitutions can be separated into common sight words and the unusual but important content words.
3. Repetitions. Repetitions can occur at all levels: word, phrase, and sentence. Repetitions are usually treated as "errors" in commerical oral reading tests except in the Diagnostic Reading Scales. Research evidence has revealed that repetitions are strategies commonly made for correcting miscues, or stalling for time to analyze preceding or succeeding words.
4. Corrections. A reader's self-corrections indicate efforts to get at meaning. The more the reader makes corrections, the greater is his maturity. Good readers make more corrections than poor readers (7).
5. Omissions and insertions. Omissions may be caused by poor word identification, carelessness, excessive speed, or poor comprehension. Good as well as poor readers make omissions. Insertions are largely due to efforts to make the text better fit the language of the reader.
6. Reversals. Reversals may occur more at the beginning reading stage, reflecting a lack of left-right orientation, but they tend to disappear as reading skills mature.

For diagnostic purposes, unrecognized words are not provided to the student in order to eliminate any influence on student's retelling or on answers to questions if comprehension is a function of oral reading.

The results of analysis on each type of miscue can be tabulated in percentages of miscues in the total number of words in the passage. This should enable the teacher to determine the appropriateness of the material for the student's performance level; the specific strategies used by the student in the reading process, including his strengths and weaknesses; and specific skills which need to be probed further.

Word Analysis Skills

If on the basis of oral reading, probing of a student's word analysis skills seems necessary, two aspects may be examined: word recognition and word identification. Diagnosis of word recognition would include words commonly used with high frequencies such as those on basic word lists. Diagnosis of word identification involves words uncommonly used which require such skills as use of phonics, structural analysis, syllabication, and context clues.

Diagnosing words in isolation by use of word lists in standardized tests or by informal measurement has been criticized. Readers often can recognize and/ or identify words in context materials but fail the same words in isolation. For diagnostic purposes, however, word lists enable the teacher to make a quick assessment on a student's use of grapheme-phoneme information. Usually a student who can recognize words in isolation can also recognize them in context, but one who recognizes words in context may fail to recognize them in word lists. The teacher needs to realize a student who can recognize words in context but not in isolation usually depends on contextual information for recognition and may lack other analysis skills.

Another use of word lists is exemplified in the Diagnostic Reading Scales by Spache (*12*). The scales have three word lists for use with students in the elementary grades. The word recognition lists serve as a pretest to indicate the best level for testing oral reading in the scales.

To diagnose word identification, a teacher may use a group phonics test such as the Doren Diagnostic Reading Test of Word Recognition Skills (Minneapolis: American Guidance Service, 1973) which samples twelve skills in second and third grade; McCullough Word Analysis Tests, Experimental Edition (Boston: Ginn, 1963), which sample eight phonic and other word analysis skills in grade four to six; or the Stanford Diagnostic Reading Test (New York: Harcourt Brace Jovanovich, 1968) Level I (grades two to four) and Level II (grades four to eight).

Individual phonics tests may be part of a test battery such as in the Diagnostic Reading Scales (with eight supplementary tests of phonic knowledge, blending, initial consonant substitution, and auditory discrimination). Spache has also offered Spelling Errors Tests as another informal approach to the diagnosis of phonic skills. The three tests are intended for grades two to four, five and six, and seven and eight (*11*: 235-246).

Intellectual Ability

Assessing the intellectual ability of a student is usually not the concern of the classroom teacher but that of the psychologist or the reading specialist. One of the major reasons is that administering individual intelligence tests such as the Weschsler Intelligence Scale for Children (WISC) or the Stanford-Binet requires special training which teachers do not normally have.

The Peabody Picture Vocabulary Test (Minneapolis: American Guidance Service, 1959) shows reasonable validity, reliability, and relationship with reading success. The test may be used for children between the ages of two years, six months to eighteen years. It has two forms that use the same set of pictures. Each form requires from ten to fifteen minutes to administer. Since this test measures vocabulary as an ability index, it may handicap persons with a language background other than standard English. Ali and Costello (1) have offered an abbreviated version which they believe eliminates cultural bias for testing some populations.

The Raven Progressive Matrices (New York: Psychological Corporation, 1938), widely used in Europe and Canada, are a series of British nonverbal tests for matching designs or design parts, or recognizing an analogy or logical sequence of designs. The tests measure general rather than verbal intelligence. There are three series: the Standard for ages eight to sixty-five, the Coloured for ages five to eleven, and the Advanced for gifted adolescents and adults. It is believed the tests are not influenced by the experiential background of the students.

Certain parts of the Detroit Tests of Learning Aptitude (Indianapolis: Bobbs-Merrill, 1968) may be used as pertinent in reading diagnosis, such as the motor speed and precision, the visual attention span for letters and for objects (for measuring visual memory), the memory for designs (for form discrimination), and the attention span for unrelated words and for syllables (for auditory attention span). The teacher may select any or all of these tests for appropriate use.

Listening comprehension level has often been used as another intelligence index which reflects the verbal ability of the student and gives clues to his potential for reading improvement. The Diagnostic Reading Scales include this as part of the standardized measurement. For an informal measure, IRI can be used. When the student reaches the frustration level in silent reading, the teacher can read the passage aloud to him. If good comprehension results, the next higher level is used for listening until comprehension also falters. In this process it should be cautioned, however, that listening comprehension is not highly correlated with silent reading. Nevertheless, the teacher can employ this index as a gross estimate about the student's potential (11:92).

References
1. Ali, Faizuniza, and Joan Costello. "Modification of the Peabody Picture Vocabulary Test," *Developmental Psychology*, 5 (July 1971), 86-91.
2. Baker, Harry J., and Bernice Leland. *Detroit Tests of Learning Aptitude.* Indianapolis: Bobbs-Merrill, 1968.
3. Barr, Rebecca. *Reading Diagnosis and Instruction.* Experimental Edition. (In process, personal communication.)
4. Betts, Emmett A. *Foundations of Reading Instruction.* New York: American Book, 1946.
5. Goodman, Kenneth S. *Miscue Analysis: Applications to Reading Instruction.* Urbana, Illinois: National Council of Teachers of English, Eric 03644, 1973.
6. Goodman, Yetta, and Carolyn L. Burke. *Reading Miscue Inventory Manual.* New York: Macmillan, 1972.
7. Liu, Stella S.F. "An Investigation on Oral Reading Miscues Made by Nonstandard Dialect Speaking Black Children," unpublished doctoral dissertation, University of California at Berkeley, 1974.
8. Potter, Thomas, and Gwenneth Roe. *Informal Reading Diagnosis: A Practical Guide for the Classroom Teacher.* Englewood Cliffs, New Jersey: Prentice-Hall, 1973.
9. Powell, William R. "The Validity of the Instruction Reading Level," in Robert E. Leibert (Ed.), *Diagnostic Viewpoints in Reading.* Newark, Delaware, International Reading Association, 1971.
10. Rupley, William H. "Standardized Tests: Selection and Interpretation," *Reading Teacher*, 26 (April 1973), 52-60.
11. Spache, George D. *Diagnosing and Correcting Reading Disabilities.* Boston: Allyn and Bacon, 1976.
12. Spache, George D. *Diagnostic Reading Scales.* Monterey: California Test Bureau, 1972.
13. Strang, Ruth. *Diagnostic Teaching of Reading.* New York: McGraw-Hill, 1969.

Informal Assessment of Comprehension: Guidelines for Classroom and Clinic

Allan Neilsen
and
Carl Braun
The University of Calgary

It seems reasonable to assume that most educators would consider comprehension to be the ultimate purpose of reading and the acme of reading performance. As is true of any psychological construct, reading comprehension cannot be observed directly but rather must be inferred from some observable behaviour that occurs during or following the reading act. One of the most common measures of comprehension is performance on questions that have been derived from the text that students have read. It is correctness of response to these questions that is often used as the only index of what has been understood during processing of the text. Since instructional intervention is presumably based on the inferences that are made about students' comprehension, it is imperative to distinguish between what actually has been comprehended and those systematic errors that result from poorly constructed test items. Therefore, it is important to be aware of the demands imposed on students by comprehension questions. Similarly, it is important to be aware of the degree to which the response demands of comprehension questions can be controlled in order to measure whether a student has abstracted the intended information from a particular passage or text.

This paper sets forth some basic considerations for assessing comprehension in the clinic and classroom. These considerations are restricted to the types of questions used to measure students' comprehension of text. Specifically, the following factors will be addressed:

a. The type of comprehension being assessed
b. The level of response required
c. The wording of questions

Examples used in the discussion are based on the following passage taken from the *Classroom Reading Inventory* (*4*):

AN UNDERWATER SCHOOL

A team of experts proved that seals had a keen sense of hearing. These men trained blind seals to expect food when they heard sounds. The seals always began snapping when a shrill signal was sounded.

It was proved that even a soft signal, a considerable distance away, could make these sea mammals respond. That should make the fisherman who splashes his oars, or talks loudly, start thinking.

The same team of experts also trained seals to recognize different sounds. One bell tone meant food; two bell tones meant no food. In the beginning, the seals made mistakes when the two bell tones were sounded. They were given a light tap after each mistake. The seals were good learners. They easily learned to tell the difference between the sounds.

What "Type" of Comprehension is Being Assessed?

Comprehension can be divided into two major domains: literal and inferential. While it might be argued that this is a too oversimplified characterization of an extremely complex phenomenon, it has the advantage of providing a basic framework that is useful for discussion. It also provides a basis for understanding more detailed systems (*2, 3*). Basically, literal comprehension involves understanding of ideas and details that are stated explicitly in the text, i.e., the information necessary to make the correct response appears in the text (see 1).

1. *What did the team of experts prove?*

Inferential comprehension, on the other hand, requires the reader to take information provided by the author and supplement it with information from *previous experience* and/or *logical reasoning*.

Inferential comprehension requires the reader to "fill in the gaps" or "read between the lines."

    2. *What evidence does the author supply that suggests that seals are intelligent?*

This distinction is not intended to be a major revelation but rather is intended to serve as a reminder that comprehension is not a global entity, making it important, therefore, to be aware of which domain we are attempting to access when we formulate questions.

A third type of question, often asked unwittingly, is one that can be answered on the basis of the reader's *world knowledge* (experience) alone without any reference to the text.

    3. *Is it possible to train seals?*

This type of question is fairly common on standardized tests (5) and can occur on teacher made tests if we don't take into account at least the general experiential background of the students being assessed. Although a detailed profile of the world knowledge of individual students is not always practical or possible, consideration of knowledge that is "typical" or "can be assumed" for a given age level should help to minimize the use of questions that do not require reading to be answered.

Lack of concern, in assessment, for what information is or is not passage-dependent leads potentially to inaccurate judgments about a student's comprehension ability. For example, Student A, drawing on his store of world knowledge responds correctly to "Is it possible to train seals?" Student B, who has not had the benefit of a trip to the zoo or even the benefit of vicarious exposure to seals in books, also responds correctly. Student B responds on the basis of the textual information, i.e., she is making an inference. The data gathered for intervention purposes are the same for the two students; both are assumed to be capable of inferring information from text. Failure to recognize the difference in sources of information that students use as a basis for response, confounds assessment procedures and, ultimately, instructional decisions based on this assessment.

What Level of Response is Required?

A second dimension of comprehension questions to be aware of is the amount of cognitive effort required to produce an answer. *Recognition, recall* and *production* questions, respectively, place increasing demands on memory. Recognition questions, which usually provide the reader with the necessary information to conduct a matching test with information held in either short term (STM) or long term memory (LTM), impose minimal demands.

4. *The seals were taught to expect a* (shock, meal, tap) *when the signal was given.*

5. *On the basis of what the writer said, which of the following statements is probably true about seals?*
   a. They are friendly
   b. They are intelligent
   c. They are almost human

On the other hand, recall questions demand that the reader rehearse (in STM) or retrieve (from LTM) information that was in the text in order to formulate an answer.

6. *Who showed that the seals have very sensitive hearing?*

7. *Why was it easy for the seals to learn the difference between sounds?*

While the type of comprehension required (literal or inferential) might be the same for both recognition and recall questions, recall questions demand more cognitive effort to answer—compare 4 and 8.

8. *What were the seals taught to expect when the signal was given?*

The hardest task is posed by a production question which requires the reader to not only reconstruct the basic information in the text but also to reorganize (analyze, synthesize, classify) and/or apply it in a new situation (find new instances of a concept, solve a problem using information from the text).

9. *Which variable in the training procedure would you say was the reinforcer?*

10. *Using the principles outlined in the passage, suggest a training program to teach a dog to "roll over."*

It is important to note that a student who is able to perform (comprehend) completely at the recognition level in either the literal or inferential domain may not be able to perform equally well *in the same material* when a recall or production response is required. The same applies to performance at the recall level relative to performance at the production level.

Failure to recognize the variation in response levels required in different tasks runs the risk of unsound instructional decision making. For example, there will be an inevitable mismatch between a student's performance on a standardized test requiring recognition level responses and the day-to-day content reading tasks making recall and production response demands. While test manual information seldom,

Neilsen and Braun

if ever, includes discussion of response levels, such information is critical to a total consideration of test validity.

The importance of test validity in relation to response levels is not restricted to standardized tests. The informal tests used in the classroom or clinic must take this into account if a precise match between assessment and instruction is to be attained. Students who spend inordinate amounts of time in the first few years of school selecting and then circling or underlining (recognition level) are unlikely to be prepared to supply unaided (recall level) information required to cope with content at increasing levels of difficulty. Such deficits must come to the fore when the students meet situations where they are required to not only recall but also to organize and produce information.

How Has the Question Been Worded?

Question stems can take one of several forms suggested by Anderson (*1*): Verbatim, transformed verbatim, paraphrase, transformed paraphrase. A *verbatim stem* uses the exact words and sentence structure that appear in the test.

11. *What did the seals always do when a shrill signal was sounded?*

It is often possible for students to respond correctly to this type of question merely by matching words from the stem with words in the text on the basis of visual memory and/or syntactic signals (when the text is not available) or direct comparison (when the text is available). Anderson argues that we need techniques for constructing questions which can be answered only if students have semantically encoded a communication, but which *cannot* be answered if they have encoded only perceptually or phonologically. He illustrates the point:

> Suppose the nonsense sentence "The sleg juped the horm" were presented. A person competent in the language could answer, "Who juped the horm?" and could also answer, "By whom was the horm juped?" but he wouldn't comprehend the message (p. 150).

In short, question 11 can be answered without reading and understanding the text. One way to counteract this is to change the syntactic structure of the stem (active to passive) so that word order cues are reduced. This is referred to as a *transformed verbatim* stem.

12. *When a shrill signal was sounded, what did the seals always do?*

While it is helpful to change the syntactic structure of the stem (active to passive) in order to reduce word order cues, the transformed verbatim stem does not totally counteract the problem. Probably the most satisfactory way to prevent responses based on visual and syntactic matching is to paraphrase the words used in the target portion of the test (that part of the text on which the question is based). This forces students to examine the meaning underlying the question and display their understanding of what was read.

> 13. *How did the seals react everytime they heard a high pitched signal?*

It is important, however, that the words used in the paraphrase have meanings that are as close as possible to the words that they are replacing. If this precaution is not taken, the resulting paraphrase might make the task more difficult, i.e., by making the intent of the question more obscure (see question 14) or actually by changing the nature of the task itself (requiring an inference instead of literal recall as in example 15).

> 14. *A high pitched signal caused the seals to react in what manner everytime they heard it?*
> 15. *Did the seals react in the same manner everytime they heard a high pitched signal?*

Guideline for the Construction of Comprehension Questions

On the basis of considerations addressed in this paper, the following guideline is suggested for the construction of comprehension questions:

1. Identify the purpose of the question (the type of comprehension it is intended to measure—literal or inferential).
2. Consider the level of response demanded by the question (recognition, recall, production).
3. Write question stems in paraphrase form (be careful not to change the meaning of the question).
4. Ensure that the correct answer requires reading and understanding of the text not a response based on previous world knowledge or visual matching alone.

References

1 Anderson, R.C. "How to Construct Achievement Tests to Assess Comprehension," *Review of Educational Research*, 42 (1972), 145-170.

2. Bloom, B., et al. *Taxonomy of Educational Objectives: Handbook I, Cognitive Domain.* New York: David McKay, 1956.
3. Clymer, T. "What Is Reading? Some Current Concepts," in H. Robinson (Ed.), *Innovation and Changes in Reading Instruction.* Chicago: National Society for the Study of Education, 1968.
4. Silvaroli, N.J. *Classroom Reading Inventory.* Don Mills, Ontario: Burns and MacEachern, 1973.
5. Tuinman, J. "Determining Passage Dependency of Comprehension Questions in Five Major Tests," *Reading Research Quarterly*, 9 (1973-1974), 206-223.

Adaptive Assessment for Nonacademic Secondary Reading

Daniel R. Hittleman
Jobs for Youth, Inc.

It is not uncommon for secondary reading teachers to use informal assessment procedures to identify students' capabilities and limitations in performing reading tasks. Quite often the Informal Reading Inventory (IRI), or the Informal Textbook Test (ITT) which consists of a so-called graded list of words and paragraphs for oral and silent reading, constitutes the informal assessment instrument. While the concept of informal assessment has validity, the idea is not tenable that one assessment instrument or that the use of one reading situation can be used to determine such things as instructional and independent and frustration levels of performance. No one assessment situation will provide complete evidence of a student's ability to read the wide range of expository and nondiscourse writing dealt with in many daily reading tasks. This is especially true of the use of the IRI with its general story, narrative passages. What is needed is not a singular measure of students' reading performances, but an adaptive means of assessing their reading performances. An adaptive assessment procedure examines reading performances with the particular materials on which one wishes to judge a student's competence.

Functional Competency and Reading

The concept of adaptive assessment is consistent with the current manner in which literacy and the reading process are being defined. For quite a while, literacy was conceived to be a score on a standardized test. As such, anyone scoring below, say, a sixth grade equivalency was deemed as illiterate. The more recent thinking on this matter is that literacy is functional—that is, literacy is determined in part by what the reader must read. Instead of there being a generalized "level of literacy," there are functional competencies which change with the reading task. The importance and implications of this will be seen as nonacademic; work related reading tasks will be examined.

The concept of functional competency and the current definition of literacy are compatible with the concept of reading as a psycholinguistic process. Within this conceptual framework, reading is an active process by which the reader reconstructs the message of the author. Rather than conceptualizing reading as an aggregate of skills, those adhering to a psycholinguistic model of reading view it as a communicative act not dissimilar from that of listening. A reader enters into a reading act with certain expectations based upon prior experiences and learnings. The printed message is examined, certain information is selected, and the reader makes a prediction about what it is the author has intended. This prediction is either confirmed or not depending upon whether the message makes sense—that is, whether the information processed from the printed page can be reconstructed into a meaningful message. If the message is confirmed (has meaning for the reader), this information becomes part of the reader's expectations and new information is selected (the reading act continues). If the message is not confirmed (has no or little meaning for the reader), additional information is selected from the printed matter so confirmation can occur. For a proficient reader, the process looks something like this:

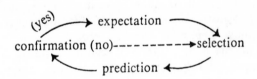

It follows then that difficulties might arise during reading for some individuals because they lack the necessary experiences and learning (expectations) to adequately select information and/or to make predictions, or the material being read does not meet the expectations the readers possess. An example of the former would be a proficient reading layperson reading a medical journal, and an example of the latter would be an author's using a syntactical structure or figure of speech that is unusual or uncommon.

Adaptive Assessment

Adaptive assessment is process oriented. It attempts to locate the quality of a reader's performance rather than just a quantification of the number and types of instances in which there is deviation from what the author intended. Adaptive assessment is analytic. It consists of steps an individual takes to continuously answer the questions:

- What has been the reader's performance in the past?
- What is the reader's performance right now?
- What might be expected of the reader in the future?

Of course, these questions must be answered about different types of reading matter; and answers cannot be extrapolated from one type of material to another without some reservations. As two materials increase in dissimilarity of content, format, and style of language, the less one can be used to predict performance on the other.

In the more traditional skill concept of reading, much of what has been said above would be classified as diagnostic. However, diagnostic teaching or the idea of diagnostic-prescriptive teaching reflects a medical viewpoint and implies the searching for factors of failure. It implies, when applied to reading instruction, a search mainly for reasons why an individual is not reading well. It seems to exclude assessing a reading performance that is not marked by failure. Adaptive assessment, on the other hand, tries to explain how a message has or has not been reconstructed without necessarily placing blame on the reader.

The performance of students' oral reading—whether it be of narrative, expository, or work related reading material—can be assessed through a process oriented procedure known as miscue analysis. A miscue is an actual oral reading response that does not match the expected response; that is, the reader orally produces a message that is not an exact reproduction of the message on the page. Through an analysis of miscues, it is possible to examine the readers' abilities to reconstruct authors' messages. It is not the number of miscues that is important to assess but the quality of the miscues. The quality of a miscue is judged by the degree to which it changes the author's intended message (2).

Miscue analyses are made by asking three groups of questions about the students' miscues:

- How effective are the students' strategies for recognizing words in context?

- How effective are the students' strategies for using their knowledge of language to realize the author's message?
- How much do the students' miscues change the intended meaning of the author?

Although miscue analysis was originally devised to assess students' reading of narrative material, research evidence shows that the same questions are effective in assessing students' reading of expository writing, and the examples below demonstrate its effectiveness in judging students' reading of work related reading materials.

Reading Materials

A good way to clarify the idea of functional competency is to examine various types of reading tasks encountered by students of high school age. Basically, much of their reading is done in prose material. In narrative material, a typical passage is

> Arthur couldn't even see the bottom of the wishing well. It was too full of paper coffee cups, ripped shopping bags, and scum. The water was so dirty he couldn't see his face. He couldn't see Mary's face either, but he knew she was looking at him by the way she was clutching his jacket at the elbow (3:157-158).

In expository writing, a passage might seem similar on the surface to narrative material, but a major difference between the two is in the organization of ideas. In the expository passage below, the information is organized to show a sequence of ideas.

> Primitive man in the New World was at first a hunter. He wandered over the land in search of rabbits, birds, turtles, and other small animals to eat. He also ate plant foods at times of the year when they grew. Occasionally he was able to kill a deer, or boar, or a bear. He used only a few simple tools and weapons.
> After about five thousand years of hunting, man became mainly a collector of plant food. Most of the plants he gathered were wild. He made choppers of stone to help him cut the plants he found. About one thousand years later, he learned to domesticate plants. These plants included corn, two kinds of squash, peas, and beans. He planted seeds and harvested his crop. Farming meant that he had to stay in one place for a certain length of time. Then he began to domesticate animals, starting with the dog.
> Man formed his first small settlements. From a hunter, to a plant collector, to a farmer, early man had now become a member of a small settled community. The beginning of civilization in the New World can be said to have started with the first small settlements (3:12).

The following passage contains two types of organization patterns. The first part of the paragraph contains an enumeration of ideas, and the second half contains a cause/result relationship.

> There are many factors that limit the growth of the rat population in a city. Rats, like people, need three main things to survive: 1) food and water, 2) shelter, and 3) a favorable climate. Rats eat the same kinds of foods that people eat. Uncovered foods and garbage are major sources of rodent food. When these are unavailable, the rats move to another area. Rodents cannot survive in cold, dry climates, and they prefer the heated environment of buildings. If it is difficult to get into buildings in one part of a city, rats will look for more favorable neighborhoods (3:99).

Other types of information organization patterns include: question/answer, comparison/contrast, generalization, and topic development (4). The manner in which the information is organized can greatly affect the efficiency with which a reader can reconstruct the author's message. When an organization pattern is unknown by the reader or is difficult to detect, a lack of reading comprehension results. Therefore, it is necessary to determine the type of organization pattern being read whenever attempting to assess a reader's ability to understand a message. Naivete on the part of a teacher commonly results in students' abilities being either over or underestimated when organization of ideas are not taken into consideration during assessment.

Job related reading tasks have their own factors of readability that are not necessarily the same as those of narrative or expository writing. On the next page are three samples of the numerous job related reading materials confronting many adolescents and young adults. The first represents the directions for an application form. This particular one is for a social security number. Other applications which young people find themselves having to read are job applications, department store credit applications, and loan applications.

SAMPLE WORK RELATED READING MATERIAL

Information Furnished on this form is CONFIDENTIAL
INSTRUCTIONS
One Number is All You Ever Need for Social Security and Tax Purposes
Special Attention Should Be Given to Items Listed Below

Fill in this form completely and correctly. If any information is not known and is unavailable, write "unknown." Use typewriter or print legibly in dark ink.

Hittleman

1. Your social security card will be typed with the name you show in item 1. However, if you want to use the name shown in item 2, attach a signed request to this form.
2. If not born in the USA, enter the name of the country in which you were born.

The second sample job related reading task is an occupation want ad. The sample copy in the ad differs in format and language from the sample application copy. Other ads which young people encounter in job related reading are telephone directory ads (indicating someone's services for hire) and general consumer ads (indicating a product for sale).

EMPLOYMENT OPPORTUNITY
NOW AVAILABLE AT THE
GRAND UNION COMPANY
3627 Erie Boulevard, E. DeWitt, New York
for an
EXPERIENCED BAKER
with management potential and ability

GRAND UNION PROVIDES
* Free Hospitalization
* Major Medical Insurance
* Free Group Life Insurance Plan
* Retirement Plan

The third sample job related reading task is from a typical invoice. A perusal of the sample invoice copy shows that the format and language of this material differ greatly from both the application and the ad.

6	dz. #2 Mongol Pcls.		8.50
100	4153 1/5 Pend.		35.10
5	#1 Blk stamp pads	1.35	6.75
300	Lt Blue 1/3 cut letter folders	8.95	26.85
3	C - 15	3.28	9.84
1	747 Stapler		10.95
3	bx Std staples	1.50	4.50
1	# 1385 File		11.25
100	5 x 8 Blank guides		4.00
			117.74
			TxEx

Each of the work related reading situations requires different reading and thinking strategies than does the reading of narrative expository writing. For example, the task for completing the application requires the following specific directions. To read the want ad requires the ability to differentiate between information indicating the job requirements and the job benefits. In reading the invoice, the task requires the understanding of abbreviations.

Assessing a Student's Reading

A reader's ability to perform the reading required in each of the job related reading situations is dependent upon that person's having the expectations to make an efficient selection of cues. The only way to determine a reader's ability to read in these situations is to actually sample the person's reading. The illustration is a portion of the protocol of a seventeen year old, out of school youth with a grade equivalency score of 5.8 on the *Adult Basic Learning Examination* (*1*), reading the work related material. It should be quite evident that the young person's proficiency varies with the reading task.

For example, on all the materials, the miscues show a fairly high graphic similarity with the text. Yet, the miscues show that the youth's ability to use language and experiential background for determining the author's message differs with the reading task and that the message has not been reconstructed uniformly across all three types of text.

In reading the instructions for a social security number, the youth creates a meaningful sentence by substituting a similar part of speech for the expected text (these/this, shall/should) or by substituting something consistent with the prior information in the sentence (print label/print legibly, shown in ink/shown in item). Where the miscue changed the author's message, corrections were made (shows/shall, tape/type). Questions asked of the youth following the reading indicate that this was considered an application for a tax number. Also, the youth generally understood what to do but did not understand the information about the use of an alternative name.

In reading the text from the want ad, the youth made few miscues that changed the meaning of the message. The words that were unknown were inferred from the other information contained in the ad and from the youth's experience in dealing with the content of other want ads. Where the meaning was substantially changed by the miscues (Era/Eric, Dead wit/De witt), the youth still knew it was an address.

In reading the text from the invoice, the youth could in no way realize the intended message since the material contained few clues that allowed for the reconstruction of a meaningful message. The youth also showed a lack of expectation (prior background information) and an inability to select appropriate information. Also, the language style of the material differed drastically from that with which the youth was familiar.

Overall, the want ad was read with the greatest relative understanding and the invoice was read with the least understanding. If this youth were to be sent out for a job in a stationery store, specific instructions to insure a readiness to perform the job related reading tasks would have to focus on the reading and writing of the special vocabulary and abbreviations used in the trade and the reading of fractions.

Summary

Adaptive assessment is an attempt to determine the quality of a reader's performance in a variety of reading situations and on a variety of written materials. It is consistent with the idea of functional competency in reading as multiple kinds and levels of literacy which are reading task specific. It is difficult to estimate a reader's competency unless that individual's reading is assessed with the particular material that is required to be read. Teachers of reading should make accommodations in their assessment procedures to determine whether a lack of communication between an author and a reader is the result of the reader's lacking knowledge and/or strategies for reconstructing the message or of the author's using a style or form of language that is unexpected under the circumstances. A reading problem, then, may result from some characteristic of the reading material and not from a factor of the reader's level of ability.

References
1. *Adult Basic Learning Examination.* New York: Harcourt Brace Jovanovich, 1967.
2. Burke, Carolyn. "Oral Reading Analysis: A View of the Reading Process," in William D. Page (Ed.), *Help for the Reading Teacher: New Directories in Research.* Urbana, Illinois: NCTE and ERIC/RCS, 1975.
3. *Cambridge Skill Power Series: Skills in Reading 1.* New York: Cambridge Books, 1972.
4. Robinson, H. Alan. *Reading and Study Strategies: The Content Areas.* Boston: Allyn and Bacon, 1975.

Psychoeducational Diagnosis as Inservice Education

Harry W. Sartain
University of Pittsburgh

Because of what we know today about individual differences in academic aptitudes, in cultural backgrounds of pupils, and in the various ways youngsters learn, many of us who work in the language arts recommend a diagnostic teaching approach in the schools. But, here, we face one of the greatest impediments to change in education—most teachers went to school in and were prepared to teach in graded schools. Therefore, a major aim of inservice education must be to help teachers learn to break away from lockstep procedures and learn the processes of personalized diagnostic instruction.

Two complex functions are included in personalized diagnostic teaching:

1. The teacher becomes thoroughly familiar with the child—personal values; family characteristics; social-emotional adjustments; aptitude patterns; and progress in every type of concept, skill, and attitude development.
2. The teacher offers differentiated instruction for individuals and small groups according to their readiness and needs for growth in each phase of the academic study, while also providing the social and emotional support that will enhance the growth of each.

In personalized diagnostic teaching the curriculum no longer is a set of inflexible annual standards. It becomes a guide for choosing and sequencing learnings in different amounts and at different rates.

Aims of Inservice Education for Personalized Diagnostic Teaching

As an introduction to inservice education for personalized diagnostic teaching, we must develop basic understandings and favorable attitudes concerning the process. Initially we need to lead teachers

1. To discover the extent of individual differences in pupil achievement, aptitude, and family backgrounds for every classroom in the school. (A good beginning is to examine pupils' subtest scores on reading and language batteries and discover the great variability within any class.)

2. To sense the need for personalized diagnostic teaching in order to provide for the great number of individual and trait differences represented in every class.

3. To understand the difference between diagnostic *progress* assessment and the traditional diagnosis of *problems*. (Diagnostic progress assessment is for everybody, not just those in trouble. It attempts to determine progress in every type of development, thereby indicating needs for continued work at a given level, or readiness to progress to the next level in a sequence of learning.)

After teachers become convinced of the need for personalized diagnostic teaching, we need to involve them in studying the ways in which the family can influence the child's education. This requires that we encourage them

4. To study the social and emotional adjustment of each child.

5. To determine the aspirations and values of their pupils.

6. To involve the parents in planning major education objectives for the school, in engaging their children in recreational activities that enhance learning, and in helping to analyze any special difficulties that their children might have in school.

At the next stage we need to develop teacher competencies in the diagnostic processes. This means that we need to make sure every teacher knows how

7. To determine the current general instructional level of each student.

8. To estimate the optimal levels of reading achievement for children in view of their aptitude and personal growth patterns.

9. To determine whether general progress is adequate, by comparing instructional level and optimum achievement level; and to develop the habit of repeating this process several times a year.

10. To make diagnostic decisions about the readiness of each youngster for the next stage of instruction and to determine the specific strengths and weaknesses in each of the component skills and capabilities for those who are having difficulty.

11. To interpret reading miscues or errors on the basis of psycholinguistic knowledge.

12. To determine whether some individuals have special perceptual modes of learning or subtle learning disabilities that necessitate major program adjustments.

The final stage of inservice development for personalized diagnostic teaching is that of preparing teachers to do differentiated teaching. Here we are concerned with helping them

13. To organize classrooms in a manner that will enable them to provide differentiated instruction in small groups or individually, both for developmental activities and corrective work.

14. To utilize varied materials and methods with the different groups according to their backgrounds, aptitudes, and needs.

15. To make additional program adaptations for individuals who have subtle learning disabilities or special styles of learning.

In this presentation I am concerned primarily with those objectives related to the diagnostic progress assessment phase of diagnostic teaching. My first purpose is to clarify the modes and levels of diagnosis.

Diagnostic Progress Assessment

Five modes of diagnosis commonly are used with school children: 1) physiological examinations; 2) informal observations of behaviors; 3) systematic observations of behaviors using scales and checklists; 4) systematic psychological probing such as attitude measures and intelligence tests; and 5) instrumental academic assessments, using such tools as achievement and diagnostic tests.

There are four levels of diagnosis in the sequence of academic progress assessment. Three of these levels involve testing and the fourth is concerned with causes of the difficulties some pupils may have.

Teachers need to learn the sequence of levels and the instruments to use in order to obtain all of the diagnostic information they need in the most efficient manner possible. This will help to prevent overtesting. And of equal importance, it will make sure they do not undertest and misdirect their teaching. The sequence leads from general to specific diagnosis.

The four levels of diagnostic progress assessment are as follows:

1. *General performance survey*—the determination of the children's general achievement levels—in this case, their reading levels. This information is needed so the teacher may judge the adequacy of the children's functioning in comparison with their estimated abilities. For this purpose, standardized norm referenced achievement tests often are used, but they must be supplemented with the teacher's informal or systematic observations of children's reading power. Standardized tests have certain values, but they do not provide the information the teacher needs to make repeated judgments about the children's levels of performance throughout the year.

2. *Diagnostic screening assessment*—the determination of students' growth profiles in the several areas of reading achievement—vocabulary, word attack skills, comprehension, reading rate, work study skills, and literary appreciation. Often it is equally important to know the children's levels of functioning in the other language arts—listening, sentence construction, informative composition, and creative writing.

Diagnostic screening in one or more phases of reading and language development should be done at the beginning of each unit of work. This will enable the teacher to decide what phases of the curriculum to emphasize next and what specific objectives to stress. It will also help the teacher to determine whether individuals have encountered learning blocks in one or more phases of study and whether they need further diagnostic evaluation.

Diagnostic screening assessment requires the use of instruments that are divided into subsections for each of the specific areas of development in reading and language. A few test batteries of this type are available, although most do not include all of the components of the reading and language program. Some teachers are able to use an individual reading inventory for part of this screening, and others may be interested in working together to construct new tests to be used within their own school.

3. *Diagnostic specification assessment*—the precise determination of every specific competency that a child has or has not attained in one of the component areas of reading or language development. It is

done only for those children who were revealed to be having special difficulty at the diagnostic screening level of assessment, and it specifies exactly what needs to be learned in order to improve performance in that phase of communication.

For example, children found to be having problems in word attack should be given a complete criterion referenced test of all of the word attack skills they might be expected to know at this stage of growth; then the teacher can specify exactly what should be taught or retaught. At another time, the screening assessment might indicate a deficiency in comprehension, so a comprehensive specification test on the various comprehension tasks should be given in order to specify what the children have not learned. Children having difficulty should be given diagnostic specification assessments in each phase of reading and language growth at different times throughout the year. It is particularly important to advise teachers that diagnostic screening and specification assessments are *not* done in one massive testing; they are done in small segments as the teacher plans for each new phase of instruction.

At present we have a number of fairly adequate diagnostic specification tests in word attack skills, and it is not difficult to test rate of reading in several types of material. We are inadequately supplied, however, with instruments for diagnostic specification assessment in other phases of reading and language growth.

4. *Diagnostic causality identification*—the determination of the underlying causes for the child's difficulty. Obviously, this assessment needs to be made only for those children involved in diagnostic specification assessments, and it may not always be necessary then.

At this point, many teachers will need an additional explanation of causality. Often, when asked why children are having difficulty in reading, teachers will respond with remarks such as, "They do not know some of the letter sounds," or "They don't seem to be able to read and remember details." These are not causes of reading difficulties. They are the difficulties in detail.

The causes of difficulties are the reasons why the detailed skills were not learned previously. Causes include such things as inadequate instruction, absence from school, social or emotional maladjustment that prevented concentration on learning, health problems, sociocultural value differences, linguistic background differences, and subtle learning disabilities. If it appears that children will be able to make adequate progress as soon as they are given corrective instruction in the specific skills that are lacking, there may be no need to spend time in identifying the original cause of the problem. But if it appears that the original cause still will block the children's learning, it is necessary to identify the cause and determine whether it can be modified or removed. Or we may determine what special instructional adaptations are needed to work around it.

One of the most effective procedures I have seen for causality identification is the psychoeducational case study conference. It was introduced many years ago at the Falk Laboratory School, University of Pittsburgh, with Dr. Benjamin Spock serving as the regular psychiatric consultant. Dr. Spock was followed by Dr. John Rinehart, who still continues in that function.

The conference is planned by the school psychologist, and a considerable number of faculty members participate. A film entitled *The Story of Stephen* illustrates how the conference is conducted and how effectively it serves as inservice education for faculty members and their professional guests. Similar conference procedures have been adopted in a number of Pennsylvania schools and, of course, other types of case studies are not uncommon elsewhere.

The Psychoeducational Case Study Conference

The case study conference brings together the child's current academic teachers, special subject teachers, former teachers, school psychologist, school nurse, and consulting psychiatrist. (Although the psychiatrist adds a particularly valuable dimension for inservice education, very worthwhile conferences can be held when a psychiatrist is not available.) Specialists such as the remedial reading teacher and the speech therapist, of course, should be included in the conference if they work with the child.

These persons from the several professions share their observations on how the child functions in different situations. By noting the patterns in behavior, they are able to reach understandings about the youngster's strengths and difficulties that no person could reach alone.

The psychoeducational conference at the University of Pittsburgh follows a fairly flexible series of steps to make sure that no important input is omitted. Before the conference convenes, the following steps are completed:

1. The teachers or the parents express great concern about the academic achievement or the social-emotional development of the youngster.

2. The teacher assembles samples of the child's pertinent school work, anecdotal notes on behavior, achievement profiles during all years in school, and other available information.
3. The teacher discusses with the principal the child's problems and achievements and a decision may be made to refer case to the psychologist for study and recommendations.
4. The psychologist studies the information, talks with teachers, and may determine that the case would be suitable for a conference. (This decision rests on how serious the problem is, how cooperative the child's parents usually are, and whether the situation includes some feature that has not been the focus of a recent conference.)
5. The psychologist obtains permission from parents for the faculty to investigate the child's problems in depth and to discuss them in a conference that is expected to produce information on how the faculty and the family can be most helpful to the child.
6. After interviews with the parents, notes are made on the histories of the child, siblings, parents, and grandparents.
7. The psychologist determines whether intelligence test information seems accurate and administers projective tests that will reveal information about the child's psychological functioning.

The conference is held at a time of day when most of the faculty members who have worked, are presently working, or will work with the child are available to attend. This sometimes occurs in the morning when student teachers are available to teach classes, or it may occur after dismissal. On some occasions, interested teachers from other schools or professionally mature student teachers and psychiatry interns are invited to observe and to participate. Leadership for the conference is assumed by the psychologist.

The conference usually proceeds for approximately an hour and a half as follows:

8. The psychologist briefly explains the reasons why the parents and teacher felt a study should be made of a particular child.
9. The child's home-room teacher, who has chief responsibility for guidance and learning, explains the problems the child seems to be having and shares information from the academic growth profiles for several years.
10. The psychologist offers the parents' views of the problem and reviews the educational, occupational, and health histories of

the child's parents, grandparents, and siblings, mentioning unusual circumstances in their lives and any problems that have affected them. The psychologist considers the history of the pregnancy and birth of the child, with the reactions expressed by the parents.

11. The nurse gives a brief health history of the child and his/her siblings taken from the school records.

12. The principal and other teachers may raise questions or inject additional information they have about the child and the family and their relationships with the school.

13. Former teachers describe the behavior and the progress as they observed it in earlier years, emphasizing information related to the current problem, and comparing past and present behaviors.

14. Teachers who work with the child in art, music, and physical education describe performance in the different fields and in response to their guidance. (This often reveals fascinating information about the child's attitudes and aptitudes in different types of activity and about differences in abilities to function under the direction of men and women authority figures.)

15. Current academic teachers may add their observations concerning the child's expression of interest in work in the special fields.

16. The psychologist explains the findings from the projective tests and points out the relationships between these observations and the child's behavior at home and responses to different teachers in different fields of activity.

17. Participants and observers raise questions to elicit additional information that they think is important or to clarify information that has been given.

18. The psychiatrist reviews significant behaviors of the child, explains how these behaviors fit into "typical" patterns of normal and abnormal behavior, and speculates on how certain patterns developed and why the child responds in certain ways. The psychiatrist often relates the child's functioning to his/her health history or to family problems.

19. Discussion continues until the causes of the problems become increasingly clear as a result of the input from all involved personnel.

20. The principal and other faculty members raise questions

about the appropriateness of instructional procedures aimed at increasing the child's competence and security, and general agreement is reached.

Of course, the parents, who are not in attendance during the professional conference, are extremely concerned about its outcome. Therefore, two more steps are taken:

21. The psychologist, or sometimes the teacher, confers with the parents to explain the findings of the case study and to recommend family practices that will be beneficial to the youngster.
22. The teacher continues to keep parents informed of the child's progress and of ways they can contribute to his/her development throughout the year.

Values as Inservice Education

As mentioned previously, the case study conference is exceptionally useful in determining the causes for pupil problems and the measures to be taken in overcoming the difficulties. In addition, it is one of the finest types of inservice education because teachers become completely absorbed in understanding and solving the problems. In the process, they learn several things much better than they would from any psychology book or course. A few of the outcomes are

1. Appreciation for the anxieties of children and parents when continuing social or educational problems are encountered.
2. Understanding of how events in children's lives from the time of their births can still have strong effects on learning and behavior.
3. Understanding of many of the patterns of normal and abnormal child behavior which can be applied in working with other children.
4. Understanding of the effects of various adult behaviors and school practices upon children's emotions and responses.
5. Appreciation for the contributions of colleagues and parents in solving children's problems.
6. An attitude of increased professionalism in working with children.

In summary, personalized diagnostic teaching requires that teachers know every child much better than has been the custom in the past and that they provide highly differentiated instruction. There is no procedure more effective in teaching teachers how to study and know children than the psychoeducational case study conference. Try it. You'll like it. And your colleagues will like you for offering them such an opportunity.

PART THREE

Suggestions for Instructional Practices

Practical Suggestions for Remedial Teachers

Albert J. Harris, Emeritus
City University of New York

This article discusses five main concerns of remedial reading teachers: How to structure the job, how to plan for efficient use of time, how to develop the right kind of relationship with pupils, how to plan for effective learning, and how to meet the demand for accountability.

Structuring the Job

For the newly appointed remedial reading teacher, or for the experienced remedial teacher assigned to a new school, the first step is to find out what policies have been established. These may include the objectives set for the remedial program, pupil selection procedures, scheduling, the size of remedial groups, the length of time a child may be kept in the program, and so forth. It is important in a new situation to adhere to the policies that have been set and to wait until one is fairly securely established in the position before working for policy changes.

Closely related to the policies issue is the need for a clear understanding of lines of authority. In different situations the nominal supervisor may be the principal or assistant principal, a district reading consultant or supervisor, a director of pupil personnel services, or a director of special education. As Humphrey (6) has pointed out, the school principal is usually the effective supervisor whose approval and support are essential. Ideally, there will be no clashes among the authorities with whom the remedial teacher has to deal. If there are, the remedial teacher needs to use every bit of tact to avoid taking sides or being caught in the middle.

Adapted from *Reading Teacher*, 30 (May 1978), 916-922.

It is also important to find out how specific the set policies are, how the supervisor envisions the job, and how open to change these ideas are. The history of special reading services in the district and in the particular school can reveal how present policies became established.

Other important questions include: What are the characteristics of the school population? What selection and evaluation procedures have been used? What pupil records are available? What use, if any, has been made of volunteers in the remedial program? How have they been recruited, trained, and supervised?

One of the first things a new teacher should do is make an inventory of materials, supplies, and equipment. Find out what there is to work with, not only in the reading room, but elsewhere in the school. Closets may be filled with discarded sets of readers and other books which may be quite useful if the children are unfamiliar with them. Idle equipment may include slide and filmstrip projectors and audio equipment that can be put to good use. A simple coding scheme can be devised to indicate the difficulty level of an item, the specific skills it seeks to develop, and whether it is for use with teacher direction or can be used independently. A separate symbol can identify game-like practice materials.

When teacher and program are continuing from the previous year, only a week may be needed to get organized; for a new teacher, a preparatory period of at least two weeks is desirable. The first priorities are pupil selection and classification. Even if this was done earlier, vacancies may need to be filled. This may involve study of pupil records, some diagnostic testing, and conferring with teachers and parents. Record folders must be set up for newly admitted pupils, and records of continuing pupils need to be brought up to date. Tentative groups should be set up and plans for some continuing pupils may be revised.

The second main activity of a preparatory period is physical arrangement of the reading center. Instructional materials need to be arranged for easy access and convenient use. A moderate amount of room decoration is desirable. Space should be arranged for group and individual activities, a listening center, a visual aids center, and a comfortable browsing area. Volunteer helpers can be quite useful in this.

Planning Efficient Use of Time

Many remedial teachers find it useful to divide the school year into four terms of approximately equal duration. In a typical school year of 190 days (or thirty-eight weeks) there can be four teaching terms of eight weeks, with one nonteaching week for preparation, testing, and conferring before each term and two nonteaching weeks at the end of the year. Alternatively, there can be two preparatory weeks at the beginning and one week at the end. It is also possible to have five or six instructional terms of shorter duration, but that may involve too many interruptions for maximum efficiency.

The duration of remedial periods usually ranges from thirty to forty-five minutes. When there are self-contained classrooms, shorter periods can be used for younger children and somewhat longer periods for older children. In departmentalized situations, the schoolwide period marked by bells usually provides the remedial teacher with five teaching periods a day plus a period for correction of tests and exercises, record keeping, instructional planning, and conferences. Often the completion of the nonteaching jobs will keep the remedial teacher busy until well after school.

Five teaching periods a day or twenty-five periods a week can best be used by having some groups twice a week and other groups three times. There is no dependable evidence that more than three remedial periods a week produce faster learning. Having five groups on three days and another five on the intervening two days is possible whether the teacher is in one school or divides time between two. The scheduling of the children should be cleared with classroom teachers to insure that no child misses too much of another important subject. Sometimes neatness of scheduling has to be sacrificed to minimize inroads into the children's other school work.

Experience has shown that highly individualized remedial teaching becomes more difficult as the size of the group increases. For the most severe disabilities it may be necessary to give completely individual help for a time, then move the child into a group of two, and later on into a larger group. Groups of five or six are probably the maximum that allow truly individual attention. Larger groups of up to fifteen are sometimes imposed on remedial teachers, but that is corrective rather than remedial teaching. The total load of a remedial reading teacher should vary between thirty-five and fifty children at any one time.

A remedial teacher can provide more individual help by using assistants. Participation of volunteers in tutoring programs has grown rapidly. Tutors can be high school students tutoring elementary school children, upper grade children tutoring children in lower grades in the same school, students in teacher education programs, parents, and senior citizens.

In 1971, Criscuolo (3) described five kinds of tutoring projects operating simultaneously in one middle sized city. He also pointed out five areas of possible difficulty: 1) training—a workshop with a minimum of five sessions is needed; 2) materials—the remedial teacher and classroom teacher provide these, but sometimes supplies are short; 3) attitude—with all good intentions, volunteers sometimes antagonize children by patronizing or critical remarks or by attitudes expressed nonverbally; 4) articulation with what the classroom teacher is doing—this is always a problem for remedial teachers and volunteers; and 5) the need for ongoing supervision and conferences between the remedial teacher and the volunteers.

In middle and secondary schools, a corps of student aides can do a variety of helpful things such as take attendance, help children find materials and put them away properly, assist children with problems, teach or supervise games, use answer keys to check exercises, and help with housekeeping (2). The effectiveness of volunteers depends mainly on the training and supervision provided. With effective use of volunteers, the amount of really individualized help that can be provided by one remedial teacher can be greatly amplified.

Developing Relationships with Pupils

One writer (6) lists the qualities of a successful remedial reading teacher as "enthusiastic, patient, optimistic, sensitive, organized, dedicated, confident, intelligent, and knowledgeable." It is significant that personality characteristics were listed first and cognitive abilities were mentioned last.

Many years ago I described the essential characteristic of the good remedial teacher as follows (4:281):

> The teacher who succeeds with poor readers must be able to convey to them the feeling that they are liked, appreciated, and understood. Each teacher must do this in ways harmonious with his own personality. A quiet teacher who creates a calm, relaxed atmosphere, a vivacious teacher who stirs children up, and a strong teacher whose self-confidence conveys a feeling of security to children, may each get fine results although their ways are different. Children know when they are liked and also have a keen sense for hypocrisy. The teacher who does not like a child usually cannot help him.

Some children, already discouraged by their previous classroom experiences, enter a remedial reading room with an attitude that seems to say, "You can't make me read." The experienced teacher counters this with an attitude that says, "I'm here to help children with reading. If you don't feel like being helped, I'll spend my time with the children who do want help." After a few sessions are spent killing time and watching what the teacher is doing with the other children, the resistant one usually begins to join in.

Teachers use what we now call "behavior modification," a technique we used to call "employing effective motivation." The procedures have changed much less than the terminology. Behavior modification involves a number of steps. First, one should establish a specific objective, such as a particular skill to be improved. Second, determine a baseline, which is the child's present level of unsatisfactory performance. Third, arrange steps to be learned in an appropriate sequence, starting with the simplest. Provide extra cues and prompts if necessary to get correct responses. Fourth, use positive reinforcement when there is a correct response. Fifth, ignore rather than punish behaviors that you do not want to be repeated. Sixth, do not attempt to reinforce every correct response; instead, reinforce frequently at first, then intermittently and at a gradually decreasing rate.

It is natural for members of a new group to be highly competitive. Some have previously learned that the only way they can win is by cheating, and some try to establish their own superiority by calling attention to blunders made by others. The teacher should accept this as normal and try to change it gradually. The teacher should repeatedly point out that all of us have had trouble in learning to read, and what counts is each one's progress, not who makes mistakes. Making mistakes is a normal part of learning. Group members are helped to construct their own progress charts and shown how to record progress. The teacher shows no interest in comparing one child's chart with another's but praises each child's improvement.

The teacher should also praise any group member who encourages or supports another member, while ignoring derogatory remarks. Gradually, the group will become more mutually supportive. It is also helpful to spend time in reading games in which chance plays a large part, so that the slowest learner will sometimes win.

Planning for Learning

Remedial reading teachers use tests for two quite different purposes. One, to measure progress, will be discussed later under accountability. The other is as a basis for planning the instructional program for each child.

Remedial teachers do not have to do elaborate testing in order to recognize children's needs and select learning activities. Each period's activities provide diagnostic information. Remedial teachers can make better use of this information than most classroom teachers for two reasons: They can focus attention on the child with much less distraction than in a large classroom, and they are trained to interpret and analyze the child's efforts. Rather than just counting right and wrong answers, the remedial teacher should explore how and why they were made. Accumulative experience with the errors makes it easier to interpret them.

One of the most useful diagnostic techniques is to ask the child to go over items again, this time thinking out loud. This can give the teacher insight into the procedures the child is trying to use, and why they do or do not work. Remedial teachers have time for this kind of qualitative analysis and should use it frequently.

Reading teachers often use an informal reading inventory to determine a child's most appropriate level for instructional and independent reading. There is, however, considerable controversy over the standards to be applied. On the whole, children in a remedial program seem to gain more from a large amount of easy reading than from a smaller amount of challenging reading. In general, materials used should result in 95 percent correct word recognition.

Sometimes a child seems unable to profit from a particular technique. The teacher should be alert to this and switch to an alternative technique.

In an efficiently planned remedial period every child is doing something useful practically all of the time. One plan for a forty to forty-five minute period that has worked well is as follows:

5 minutes	Assignments, getting materials, cleaning up.
10 minutes	Teacher-led group lesson, often introducing a new subskill.
15 minutes	Follow-up exercise to give practice in applying the group lesson. Teacher has time to work individually with two or three children.
10 minutes	As children finish the follow-up exercise, they move to an individual activity, often self-chosen from several options.

This plan allows for considerable flexibility. A child who does not need the group lesson may be excused and have more time for individual activities. A follow-up exercise may be omitted on some days to allow the teacher time to read an exciting story to the group or to work with individual children.

Meshing with the Curriculum

Many children have had their growing self-confidence shattered when, after trying hard in a remedial program and making apparent progress, they were told at the end of the year that they would have to repeat the grade because of failure in other subjects. This is all the more tragic because so often it can be prevented.

As a first step, the remedial teacher should consult with other teachers on how to schedule the children so as to interfere as little as possible with other important subjects. Second, discussions can be held with teachers on how the remedial teacher can help in the content areas. This may bring out such ideas as getting someone to read assignments to children at home or in school, finding alternative easier texts and references for children to use, recording a text on tape or cassette for children to listen to, and testing poor readers orally instead of in writing. As children near normal grade level in general reading ability, their remedial program can be modified to provide training in how to master technical vocabulary and how to get as much information as possible from difficult books. Specific help can be given on such matters as how to read an arithmetic problem or how to study required spelling words.

If a remedial pupil's promotion is in question, the remedial teacher should be objective in trying to predict the probable outcome of promotion or nonpromotion. If it seems probable that with continued help in the remedial program the child will be able to do passable work in the next grade, a persuasive argument can be made for promoting the child.

Accountability and Remedial Reading

With educational budgets now under sharp scrutiny, remedial reading programs must expect to be challenged to demonstrate their worth. In the past, many remedial teachers have felt that time taken for systematic retesting could better be spent in teaching. Such an attitude is no longer practicable. Retesting at appropriate intervals is necessary to demonstrate the value of the program.

Standardized tests are better suited than informal or criterion referenced tests for periodic measurement of progress. Equivalent forms make it possible to retest without repeating the same items. The testing should include tests of word recognition, accuracy in oral reading, and comprehension in silent reading. The grade scores on standardized tests are easily explained to parents, school board members, and other concerned laypersons. The gain score obtained by subtracting a pretest score from the posttest score after a period of remedial help is also a simple concept. The gain score can be easily converted into a percentage of normal progress and compared with the percentage of normal progress of the same children before entering the remedial program.

For example, Ted, a fourth grader, was pretested in September, entered the remedial program two weeks later, and was retested in June. His average reading grade was 2.7 in September and 3.9 in June. If we count the remedial period as a full year, his gain was 1.2 and his percentage of normal progress was 120. Before the fourth grade he had had 3 years of reading instruction; his September grade score of 2.7 represented 1.7 years of progress in those three years. (It is essential to remember that the grade score scale starts at 1.0, not at zero.) Thus Ted's previous rate of progress was 1.7 divided by 3, or 57 percent. His remedial progress of 120 percent was, therefore, twice his previous rate of progress. However, entering fifth grade with a reading grade of 3.9 meant that he was probably not ready to be discharged from the remedial program, unless the fifth grade teacher would be able to give him the help that he would still need.

For those who want a measure of improvement that takes the child's learning potential into account, the Reading Expectancy Quotient may be used (5). A Reading Expectancy Age is found by combining the child's mental age with his/her chronological age. Reading age divided by expectancy age gives a quotient which is near 100 for those making normal progress and below 90 for those with reading disabilities. Satisfactory progress is shown when the child's Reading Expectancy Quotient is higher after a period of remedial help than before remediation.

Some measurement specialists (9, 10) have criticized the methods just described on the ground that they do not allow for regression effects. A regression toward the mean tends to occur when pupils with high or low scores are retested with an equivalent test; the retest scores tend to be closer to the mean. An alternative is to compute an expected score from a regression equation and compare the retest score with that expected score. However, children who are not given remedial help just do not regress toward the mean; instead, they tend to fall farther and farther behind. The expected score from a regression equation sets an unrealistically high expectation and, in some cases, can turn a real gain in reading into a theoretical loss.

The challenge for accountability is often met by comparing children's status at the time of leaving the remedial program with status before entering it. We have, unfortunately, very few reports on the long term effects of remedial reading instruction. These few seem to indicate that the results of short term remedial help tend to fade out. Children given long term help of two or three years, however, tend to continue to improve (1), and some of them can go on to meet the challenges of college and graduate school (8, 7).

It seems probable, therefore, that discharging pupils from a remedial reading program before they are ready may, in the long run, defeat the aims of the program. Programs which arbitrarily limit a child's attendance to eight or sixteen weeks must be challenged to show they provide lasting benefits.

I suggest two criteria for judging whether a child is ready to succeed without further remedial help. The first is ability to read required assignments in the regular program with passable comprehension. The second is the establishment of the habit of doing some reading for pleasure, thus continuing to practice the new skills. If both of these conditions have been met, continuing progress can be expected; with either missing, progress in reading may well come to a halt when remedial help is stopped.

There are other indicators of the success or failure of a remedial program besides the reading gains of the children. They include such diverse items as attendance records; frequency of disciplinary infractions; continuation in school beyond the compulsory attendance age; teacher ratings of work, effort, and personality; ratings and reports by parents; and self reports and ratings by the pupils. All of these can provide information on the success of the remedial program. A remedial program is easily crossed out of a budget, and facts are needed if it is to be convincingly justified.

One final suggestion: Knowing general principles such as those discussed in this article is important, but learning when and how to apply them does not come overnight. Specific situations have special characteristics that need to be taken into consideration. For remedial teachers, as for remedial pupils, mistakes are a normal and necessary part of the learning process. A successful remedial teacher is alert to evidence on what is working well and what is not. This may come from the reactions of the pupils, their parents, or their classroom teachers. Becoming aware of a problem is the first step toward its solution. The successful remedial teacher is continually appraising every aspect of the program and trying to make adjustments that will produce still better results.

References

1. Balow, Bruce, and M. Blomquist. "Young Adults Ten to Fifteen Years after Severe Reading Disability," *Elementary School Journal*, 66 (1965), 44-48.
2. Crawford, Gail, and Dick Conley. "Meet You in Reading Lab," *Journal of Reading*, 15 (October 1971), 16-21.
3. Criscuolo, Nicholas. "Training Tutors Effectively," *Reading Teacher*, 25 (November 1971), 157-159.
4. Harris, Albert J. *How to Increase Reading Ability*, Third Edition. New York: Longmans, Green, 1956.
5. Harris, Albert J., and Edward R. Sipay. *How to Increase Reading Ability*, Sixth Edition. New York: David McKay, 1975.
6. Humphrey, Jack W. "Remedial Programs: Can They Be Justified?" *Journal of Reading*, 15 (October 1971), 50-53.
7. Rawson, Margaret B. *Developmental Language Disability: Adult Accomplishments of Dyslexic Boys.* Baltimore, Maryland: The Johns Hopkins Press, 1968.
8. Robinson, Helen M., and Helen K. Smith. "Reading Clinic Clients: Ten Years Later," *Elementary School Journal*, 63 (1962), 22-27.
9. Thorndike, Robert L. *The Concepts of Over- and Underachievement.* New York: Teachers College Press, Columbia University, 1963.
10. Yule, William, and Michael Rutter. "Epidemiology of Social Implications of Specific Reading Retardation," in Robert M. Knights and Dirk J. Bakker (Eds.), *The Neuropsychology of Learning Disorders: Theoretical Approaches.* Baltimore, Maryland: University Park Press, 1976, 25-39.

Sentence-Combining Practice Aids Reading Comprehension

Warren E. Combs
University of Georgia

Research emphasizes the need to integrate instruction in the various forms of language communication—reading, writing, speaking, and listening (*21, 8*). However, the studies seldom lead to definable classroom procedures for the reading teacher. Instead, one most often finds general statements to the effect that practice in one language form enhances one of the other forms. For example, Fox (*8*:670) says: "In essence, surrounding children with a wealth of oral language, meaningful for them both to hear and use seems to be a simple but significant step in a process that will culminate in an introduction and mastery of another language form: the written word."

The prospects are exciting: Teachers could present written or oral exercises with the satisfaction of knowing that equal time need not be given to reading and listening activities. It is unfortunate, however, that statements like Fox's are found at the conclusions of articles, leaving implementation entirely to the classroom teacher.

This article describes the general nature of learning activities alluded to by such sources and illustrates an instructional procedure that already has accumulated impressive theoretical and empirical research support. For the description of the general learning tasks, I depend upon Cazden's final chapter of *Child Language and Education* (*2*), although complementary sources exist (*1, 2*). The instructional procedure, sentence-combining practice, is extensively described

Adapted from *Journal of Reading*, 21 (October 1977), 18-24.

elsewhere (*14, 23*); thus I will pay special attention to its application to reading instruction.

Cazden focuses on the nature of classroom learning experiences and casts them into three broadly defined, but discretely illustrated, categories: learning that, learning to, and learning how.

Briefly, "learning that" requires that the student have conscious knowledge about language, its nature (including parts of speech), its theoretical structure, and its use. "Learning that" is often labeled "linguistics," the scientific study of language and must be studied for its own sake. Research shows no positive correlation between "learning that" knowledge of language and improvement in the communication forms. Research does, however, indicate some negative correlation between "learning that" study and children's attitudes toward school and language classes themselves (*7*).

Cazden describes "learning to" activities as the general learning tasks that encourage a "critical skill" (spelling, pronunciation, vocabulary choice) to become a consistent pattern of behavior. "Learning to" is often labeled "learning by doing" and such approaches have worked well in the alternative schools (*9*); they have also appeared in suggestions for regular school activities (*6*).

"Learning how" appears to be a hybrid form of learning, encouraged by and appropriate for the artificial environment of the classroom. Its purpose is to present exercises that provide students extensive practice in performing certain individual critical skills that, when combined with other skills, constitute a "facility," such as one of the language forms (*20*).

From Cazden's categories and subsequent descriptions, then, "learning to" experiences seem the most effective kind of learning, "learning that" the least connected to improvements in communication, and "learning how" the most appropriate to classroom constraints as they now exist. More simply, "learning to" situations, though preferred, cannot be sustained in typical classroom situations; "learning that" experiences are extra fare; and "learning how" experiences must carry a healthy proportion of the learning activity.

"Learning how" activities proliferate since they are easy to fabricate. One need only pick up any basal reading series or beginning language arts text to notice the torrent of drills, pattern practices, and workbook exercises of basic skills that fill the pages, claiming to supply the extra push toward reading enjoyment for the student. But "learning how" exercises that actually bolster improvements in reading or writing (in a testable fashion) are not abundant.

The improvement in a critical skill (for example, syntactic flexibility) must translate into an improved facility (reading or writing). Sentence-combining practice is one instructional procedure that does so translate and thus, both from a theoretical and practical point of view, it should be considered a serious part of intensive language experience in reading instruction.

A Study of Interaction

Sentence-combining exercises were developed in the early sixties by several applied linguists who drew upon systematic processes of combining "kernel" sentences in a manner similar to that used by Chomsky in his transformational grammar (12, 11). They constructed the exercises much like a mathematical problem, starting with the main kernel sentence and then listing all other kernels to be added. Students would begin with the first kernels in an additive fashion, depending on parenthetical signals and their own linguistic intuitions for guidance. For example, exercise A results in B.

A. Professor Dingle could see SOMETHING.
   Sam did not understand SOMETHING. (THAT)
   The poem was about something. (WHAT)

B. Professor Dingle could see that Sam did not understand what the poem was about.

Research indicates that written and oral sentence-combining practice affects students' writing abilities. Following extensive sentence-combining practice, students write stories and essays that 1) consist of significantly more mature sentences, 2) are judged by teacher-raters to be of significantly better quality, and 3) show qualitative and quantitative superiority even eight weeks after formal instruction has ceased. It is important to note that the results from qualitative measures allayed earlier fears that sentence-combining practice would encourage overcomplicative syntax. Therefore, sentence-combining practice equipped students with mature strategies they employed when needed.

A study was done to determine if the positive effects of sentence-combining practice transferred to reading comprehension (4). Educational theory suggests it would (23). The reasoning is as follows: Coleman (3) found that syntactic difficulty in reading passages affects students' comprehension of those passages. Thus, it seems logical that as students' abilities to handle more difficult syntax increases, they will score higher on comprehension tests of more difficult passages.

The Combs design to measure this included a pre and posttest version of a specially constructed reading measure adapted from the Rate and Comprehension Check Tests of the Baldridge Reading Instruction Materials, junior high and entering college levels. Between the two testings, students in the experimental group received sentence-combining instruction aimed at increasing ability to handle complex syntactical structures.

The pre and posttest reading measure was constructed from two readings from the Baldridge tests that were roughly the same length (1,005 and 985 words) at an entering college level (grades 11-13) and at similar levels of syntactic complexity (22.3 versus 20.9 words per T-unit, and 13.9 versus 13.13 words per clause).

Hunt (*10*) indicates that the production level of high school graduates is about 18 words per T-unit and 10 words per clause; since receptivity precedes productive ability, the selections were considered difficult but appropriate for seventh graders to read, and the content was also fo sufficient interest to warrant their use with these students. The study indicated that the students in the experimental and in the control group were not significantly different in terms of reading rate and comprehension on the pretest.

Analysis of the results showed that after sentence-combining practice, the experimental group experienced significant gains in reading comprehension scores. Reading rate was not significantly affected. ANOVA lucidly illustrated the significant contrast by groups (posttest experimental M = 3.67, $F(1) = 12.97$, $p < .001$).

There were limitations to the study. Absolute reliability for the special reading measure could not be claimed since the passages were not written for this experimental population and thus were not finely enough calibrated to insure certainty. But it is important to note that the study has illustrated empirically the interaction between gains in various forms of the language arts. Further work should investigate whether sentence-combining affects other language forms as it apparently does reading. Studies using other types of syntactic practice, too, might deliver empirical confirmation of significant reading gains from various oral and written exercises which could revolutionize reading instruction.

Practicing Sentence-Combining

A wide range of sentence-combining activities are available to reading instructors. Most are for intermediate grade readers and secondary readers in need of remediation.

Since sentence-combining practice attracts even unmotivated students, the teacher could base sentence-combining activities on a reading passage and use them as an alternative to answering questions at the end of an assignment. A graduate student of mine successfully helped her "special" twelfth graders through the novel *Jaws* in this fashion and reported more informed discussion from the point at which she began sentence-combining exercises. She modified the basic sentence-combing problem by omitting a crucial word or two and employed the result as a quiz over a single chapter:

a) Brody removed the lid.
b) The lid was on the garbage can.
c) Sean's _____ was lying there.
d) The _____ was in a twisted heap.
e) The heap was on top of a pile of garbage.
Brody removed the lid of the garbage can and discovered Sean's body in a twisted heap on top of a pile of garbage.

The exercise required the students to read the assigned chapter and gave them practice in writing out a resume of it while relieving them of the overburdening pressures of spelling, punctuation, and word choice.

A sequence of sentence-combining problems could also serve as enticement for reluctant students to read further in extended stories or short novels. One could base the sequence, for example, on the narrative line of the low vocabulary-high interest novelette *A Choice of Weapons (16)*. The following example includes four of a series of ten such exercises:

5. I spent the next few nights sleeping on trolley cars. The rent was reasonable. (BECAUSE)
6. I thought a lot about SOMETHING. I was going to get by somehow. (HOW)
   I even considered robbery. (AND)
7. One morning on the trolley I woke to find SOMETHING.
   I was all alone with the conductor. (THAT)
8. My hand tightened around the switchblade SOMETIME.
   The switchblade was *in my pocket.*
   I saw the bundle of green bills. (WHEN)
   He held the bills in his hand. (WHICH/THAT)

Such an activity would, of course, require some instruction in a signal system somewhat like O'Hare's, but it need not be as extensive as his *(15)*.

Exercises could be completed orally much like the following one based on Moffett's naturalistic dialogues *(13)*. The activity requires that students form groups of three. Student A is to make a declarative statement based on recently read materials and provide any additional information requested. B is to request more information: Where? Which one? Why not? Never? Are you sure? Who's he? and then join all the information together in a single statement. C is to referee the dialogue, writing down the finished product. The groups may wish to compete with others in the class to see which group produces the "best" sentences. Roles should be switched within the group to allow each student oral and written practice.

Another oral activity requires an impromptu production of a class sentence based on materials recently read. It is helpful to place a large posterboard with a list of signals for complicating the sentence ("which, that, how, even though, after") in a prominent place in the classroom. Set up a round robin session in which a student begins by thinking of a sentence but placing only the first word of it on the board. A second student adds a second word, a third yet another, and so on. The activity continues until the group judges that the sense of the sentence has been blurred. Dividing the class into two groups and letting them compete in producing the larger sentences works well.

Perron (*17, 18*) lists a number of other games and activities: sentence-combining poems, sentence partners, sentence-combining bean bag, sentence-combining concentration, sentence-combining tennis. His creative variations suggest, however, that one might consider any number of games as framework for extensive sentence-combining practice. The singular requirement of the activities is that they insure that students become intently involved in producing complex sentences.

One exercise that is quite simple to construct is patterned after the old-fashioned spelldown. The room is divided into two teams; each team member attempts in turn to score for his side and if he fails, the turn moves to the next in line on the opposing side. Two differences, however: the task is a sentence-combining problem and there are at least three levels of difficulty. Be certain to assign a different point value to the levels (one through three) and stop each student at the very point he makes a mistake in the sentence-combining problem. The first rule is only fair and the second helps give the other students a clue to the correct combination.

Since the instructor chooses the problems or constructs them for the activity (*5*), no student is overcome by difficulty of the task and all listen intently to one another since the problem may be theirs if an opponent fails the task.

Another activity follows the rules of dominoes as closely as possible. The "dominoes" are rectangular cards divided in half by a line across the middle; each half contains a numeral and a simple sentence that can be combined with any other sentence accompanied by the same numeral (see illustration).

Sentence-Combining Dominoes Game

4	6	6	6	5
		Not a teacher missed the game.		
Frieda had a million freckles.	The game pitted the two bottom teams.	6	The game was rescheduled at South High Stadium.	Mrs. Campbell rules the lunchroom with an iron hand.
		The game had some bizarre attraction.		

Number combinations needed on dominoes: 6/6 6/5 6/3 6/2 6/1 6/0
5/5 5/4 5/3 5/2 5/1 5/0
4/4 4/3 4/2 4/1 4/0
3/3 3/2 3/1 3/0
2/2 2/1 2/0
1/1 1/0
0/0

A dealer shuffles the cards (twenty-eight in a deck using the numerals zero through six), deals seven to each of three players, and places the remaining seven in a "bone pile." He then asks the player with the largest double (a domino with the same numeral in each half) to play. To complete his turn, the first player must combine the two sentences on his domino. If he does so to the satisfaction of his opponents, he scores the sum of the two numbers on the domino. A double six domino, for example, is worth twelve points. The second player may then place a domino containing a six next to any of the four sides of the double six and score by combining the sentences in the halves that touch. If she plays her six off the side of the double six and satisfactorily combines both the #6 sentences from the double with the #6 sentence on her own domino, she receives eighteen points; if she places it at the end, she could score only twelve points.

Combs

Unless a double is being used, dominoes are placed end to end and the players combine and receive points for the two sentences that touch. Play continues until one player runs out of dominoes. If any player has no domino with the required numeral, he must draw dominoes from the "bone pile" until he gets one that allows him to complete his turn. All scoring is subject to the approval of the opponents. And at game's end, all players with unplayed dominoes must total up those points and give them to the one who "played out" first. If no one player can "play out," the game is ended with each player subtracting the points in his hand from his total.

A set of dominoes may be constructed in several ways, but I used posterboard and cut the dominoes 2¾″ x 5½″ (about 7 by 14 cm). In this way, the sentences were easily read and the game could be played on either a large table or the floor. Lamination with plastic protects the cards from excessive wear.

Many other games exist, available for adaptation to sentence-combining practice: hangman, crossword puzzles (cross sentence puzzles, that is), and several kinds of card games. In all cases, students would be motivated to produce relatively complex sentences and gain confidence in their judgments of acceptable linguistic performance of their peers.

References
1. Britton, James. "Talking to Learn," *Language, the Learner, and the Schools*. A research report by Douglas Barnes with a contribution from James Britton and a discussion document prepared by Harold Rosen on behalf of the London Association for the Teaching of English. New York: Penguin Books, 1971, 79-116.
2. Cazden, C.B. "On Language Education," *Child Language and Education*. New York: Holt, Rinehart and Winston, 1972, 236-247.
3. Coleman, E. B. "The Comprehensibility of Several Grammatical Transformations," *Journal of Applied Psychology*, 48 (1964), 186-190.
4. Combs, W. E. "Further Implications and Effects of Sentence-Combining Exercises for the Secondary Language Arts Curriculum," *Dissertation Abstracts International*, 36 (1975), 1266A.
5. Cooper, C.R. "An Outline for Writing Sentence-Combining Problems," *English Journal*, 62 (1973), 96-102, 108.
6. Dunning, Stephen. "Needed: Modest Rebels," a report of the Fifth Annual Conference on the Teaching of the English Language Arts. Athens: Language Education Department, University of Georgia, 1976, 1-7.
7. Elley, W.B., et al. "The Role of Grammar in a Secondary School English Curriculum," *Research in the Teaching of English*, 10 (Spring 1976), 5-21.

8. Fox, S. E. "Assisting Children's Language Development," *Reading Teacher*, 29 (April 1976), 666-670.

9. Greenberg, A. "City-as-School: An Approach to External Interdisciplinary Education," *English Journal*, 65 (October 1976), 60-62.

10. Hunt, K.W. *Grammatical Structures Written at Three Grade Levels*, NCTE Research Report No. 3. Urbana, Illinois: National Council of Teachers of English, 1965.

11. Mellon, J.C. *Transformational Sentence-Combining*. NCTE Research Report No. 10. Urbana, Illinois: National Council of Teachers of English, 1969.

12. Miller, B.D., and J.W. Ney. "Oral Drills and Writing Improvement in the Fourth Grade," *Journal of Experimental Education*, 36 (1967), 93-99.

13. Moffett, J. *Drama: What Is Happening. The Use of Dramatic Activities in Teaching of English*. Urbana, Illinois: National Council of Teachers of English, 1967.

14. O'Hare, F. *Sentence-Combining*. NCTE Research Report No. 15. Urbana, Illinois: National Council of Teachers of English, 1973.

15. O'Hare, F. *Sentencecraft*. Lexington, Massachusetts: Ginn, 1975.

16. Parks, Gordon. *A Choice of Weapons*. New York: Harper and Row, 1966.

17. Perron, J.D. "An Exploratory Approach to Extending the Syntactic Development of Fourth Grade Students through the Use of Sentence-Combining Methods," *Dissertation Abstracts International*, 35 (1975), 4316A.

18. Perron, J.D. "Beginning Writing: It's All in the Mind," *Language Arts*, 53 (September 1976), 652-657.

19. *Rate and Comprehension Check Tests*. Junior high and entering college levels. Greenwich, Connecticut: Baldridge Reading Instruction Materials, 1966.

20. Scheffler, I. *Conditions of Knowledge*. Glenview, Illinois: Scott, Foresman, 1965.

21. Simms, Eunice. "Communication Skills," a report of the Fourth Annual Conference on the Teaching of the English Language Arts. Speech presented at the Fourth Annual Conference on the Teaching of the English Language Arts. Athens: Language Education Department, University of Georgia, 1975, 21-25.

22. Steinmann, Martin, Jr. "Rhetoric Research," *The New Rhetorics*. New York: Charles Schribner's Sons, 1967, 16-32.

23. Stotsky, S.L. "Sentence-Combining as a Curriculuar Activity: Its Effect on Written Language Development and Reading Comprehension," *Research in the Teaching of English*, 9 (Spring 1975), 30-71.

What Every Teacher Should Know about Myopia

Delwyn G. Schubert
California State University at Los Angeles

Myopia (nearsightedness), second only to astigmatism in its incidence as a visual defect, threatens an increasing number of young people yearly. The inability to clearly see distant objects has been a matter of major concern to eye specialists for many years. A great deal of research continues in this area.

The Nature and Incidence of Myopia

Myopia is positively associated with good reading and is characterized by an elongated eyeball (6). Distant objects come to a focus in front of the retina and appear blurred. And while it may be argued that a myope has to make less accommodative effort to bring the printed page into focus, the condition is not necessarily desirable. Any amount of the defect appears to enhance the possibility of retinal detachment which can lead to blindness (7).

Myopia is rarely found at birth and is seldom found among those who are under six years of age. Most myopia becomes noticeable after a child reaches the fifth or sixth grade. As schooling continues, the incidence of the defect increases. Girls show a greater amount of myopia than boys and tend to develop it earlier (7). About 8 percent of children in the elementary grades are myopic, 10-15 percent are found at the junior high school level, 15-25 percent in high school, 25-50 percent in college, and 40-60 percent in graduate school.

Causes of Myopia

Everyone agrees that myopia is hereditary or acquired. But there is no agreement as to the degree to which each of these factors is involved. In recent years, however, a wealth of experimental evidence has given added credence to the contention that environmental forces are extremely potent causes of myopia. For example, Young (9, 10, 11) has shown that primates whose eyes are very similar to the eyes of humans develop myopia under controlled experimental conditions that restrict visual space to a distance under 20 inches. Studies of Eskimos at Barrow, Alaska (12) reveal that among the oldest generation there is no myopia. In the second generation, myopia appears among the younger persons about 21 percent of the time. And in the third generation, an amazing 62 percent of those between eleven and twenty-five years of age evidence the defect. Attributing these differences to hereditary changes over three generations would seem untenable. The explanation is that with increased schooling nearpoint demands gradually bring about a stretching or elongation of the eyeball (7).

Eye Glasses and Myopia

Concave lenses have been the traditional prescription for a myope whose elongated eyeballs result in rays of light from distant objects coming to a focus before reaching the retina. But there is a danger. A myope who is fitted with concave correction for distant vision will restimulate the accommodative process which caused an elongation of the eyeball if he/she wears the lenses for reading at nearpoint (7). A fairly recent study by Young (5) proves that myopic children who are provided with bifocals which reduce the accommodative response at reading distance show a significant reduction in the rate of the development of myopia.

Prevention of Myopia

There are a number of things a teacher can do that should be part of a program stressing prevention of myopia. These are as follows:

1. Instruct children that proper reading distance is equal to the length of the arm from knuckles to elbow. This is referred to as Harmon distance and is equal to thirteen to sixteen inches (1).

2. Improve children's writing posture by having writing surfaces at elbow height. To ensure proper pencil grip and more seeing room, put

a rubber band on the end of the pencil about one inch from the writing tip. Proper posture and proper pencil grip make it easier for children to maintain Harmon distance when writing. Children endeavoring to write with their heads at four to eight inches from their papers (frequently associated with myopia) function with a focusing stress of two to six diopters over the three diopters required at thirteen inches (2).

3. Encourage children to tilt their books when reading. (A bookholder is strongly recommended.) If a book lies flat on a desk or lap during reading, several times more stress is placed on the eyes when viewing the lower part of a page as compared to the top of a page (4). In addition, the mere act of bending over a book for long periods may result in eyeball elongation because of gravitational pull (3).

4. Encourage children to look up at a distant object at the end of reading each printed page. This allows for relaxation of the focusing mechanism that can cause myopia when it is forced to remain active over long periods of time.

5. Encourage children to read in a good light. Dim or insufficient lighting is conducive to myopia (4).

6. Discourage children from engaging in nearpoint activity for extended periods of time when they are sick. During a weakened condition, undue strain of the accommodative mechanism may be damaging.

7. Encourage parents to have their children's eyes checked as often as practical so any tendency toward myopia can be caught in its incipient stages. Vision therapy and/or the new science of orthokeratology are more effective in combating myopia if the condition is not too advanced.

8. Special attention should be given to children who already wear glasses. Those whose correction is for myopia* should be asked whether they have been told by their doctor to wear their glasses for reading and other nearpoint work. (If a child does not know, it is advisable to ask the parents to check with the vision specialist.) This is important because, as indicated earlier in this paper, there is strong evidence that the myope who wears glasses at nearpoint will restimulate the accommodative mechanism, thus causing the development of a greater amount of myopia.

---

*The simplest way for a teacher to spot a correction for myopia is to sight on a distant object while looking through the child's glasses. If the distant object recedes or looks smaller, the child is wearing concave lenses. Concave lenses constitute a correction for myopia.

References
1. Harmon, Darell B. *The Coordinated Classroom*. Austin, Texas: American Seating Company, 1951.
2. Kahn, Ernest J. "Handwriting and Vision," *Journal of the American Optometric Association*, 40 (1969), 1-6.
3. Levinshon, G. *Die Ent Stehung der Kurzsichtigkeit*. Berlin: S. Karger, 1912.
4. Nolan, J.A., and R.L. Van Lanningham. "Myopia Prevention," *Myopia Control* (an undated and noncopyrighted optometric brochure).
5. Oakley, Kenneth, and Francis A. Young. "Bifocal Control of Myopia," *American Journal of Optometry and Physiological Optics*, 52 (1975), 758-764.
6. Thompson, Leslie. *Improve Your Eyesight Naturally*. London: Thorsons Publishers, 1956, 40.
7. Young, Francis A. "The Nature and Control of Myopia," *American Journal of Optometry*, 48 (1977), 451-457.
8. Young, Francis A. "Myopia and Personality," *American Journal of Optometry*, 44 (1967), 192-201.
9. Young, Francis A. "Development and Retention of Myopia by Monkeys," *American Journal of Optometry*, 38 (1961), 545-555.
10. Young, Francis A. "The Effect of Restricted Visual Space on the Primate Eye," *American Journal of Ophthalmology*, 52 (1961), 799-806.
11. Young, Francis A. "Heredity and Myopia in Monkeys," *Optometric Weekly*, 57 (1966), 44-49.
12. Young, Francis A. "Development of Optical Characteristics for Seeing," in Francis A. Young and Donald B. Lindsley (Eds.), *Early Experience and Visual Information Processing in Perceptual and Reading Disorders*. Washington, D.C.: National Academy of Sciences, 1970, 35-61.

Teaching Reading to the Hearing-Impaired Child

Judy I. Schwartz
Queens College, CUNY

His name was Jimmy. I remember my sense of apprehension when I saw that name included in my first grade roster. It was not because he was older than the others, having spent two years in kindergarten, or that he was noticeably bigger. Jimmy was deaf. How, I wondered, could I help this child? How, indeed, could I cope with his handicap?

Because of recently enacted federal legislation which requires that children with handicapping conditions receive their education in the "least restrictive environment" more children like Jimmy will be found in regular classrooms. More teachers will be faced with the responsibility of teaching them. This does not mean wholesale abandonment of hearing-impaired and other handicapped children from the special resources available to them in the past. It does mean that such children will be spending more of their school time in regular classes. Here they will continue, in most cases, to receive direct assistance from specially trained persons on a part-time basis or indirect assistance via the classroom teacher who, in turn, will receive instruction and help from the special teacher serving as a resource person. In any event, the regular classroom teacher will have increased responsibility in the education of the hearing-impaired child.

Hearing-impaired is a generic designation indicating a continuum of hearing loss from mild to profound. The hearing loss is measured in decibels (dB) which is the unit used to measure the relative intensity of sound. Following are the categories of hearing-impairment:

Reprinted with permission from *Reading Horizons*, Vol. 18, No. 4 (Summer 1978), 249-257.

mild—loss of 27-40 dB; *moderate*—loss of 56-70 dB; *severe*—loss of 71-90 dB; and *profound*—loss of more than 90 dB. Possibly because of better nutrition and more effective treatment of infectious diseases, there are fewer deaf children today than in the past. There are also fewer so-called "normal deaf," those without additional handicapping conditions. The rubella epidemic of several years ago produced children with various combinations of orthopedic, visual, auditory, and other categories of handicapping conditions. However, the single most serious impediment to successful school achievement in general and to learning to read in particular is the deaf child's impaired language function.

The Problem

Studies of the academic achievement of the deaf invariably find a serious educational lag when compared to the hearing population. Dale (*2*) estimates that normally hearing children may have a speaking vocabulary of some 2,000 words by the time they enter kindergarten. The deaf may use only 250 words by the same age. The problem appears to become accelerated with increasing age. Rosenstein and MacGinitie (*17*) note that younger deaf children outperform older deaf children proportionately. Hargis (*9*) reports a discrepancy of approximately eight years between the mean reading achievements of hearing and deaf children when the comparison is made after the completion of their regular educational programs. Wrightston, Aranow, and Muskovitz (*21, 22*) used the Metropolitan Achievement Tests to study the performance of over 5,000 deaf children in 73 school programs of various kinds in Canada and the United States. They found that the children's average gain in reading achievement in the age span of ten to sixteen years was less than one year. The sixteen year olds were found to have an average reading achievement grade of 3.5. Hammermeister (*8*) used the Stanford Reading Achievement Test to measure the performance of deaf adults who had completed their education at a residential school seven to thirteen years earlier. Significant gains were made on word meaning but not on the test of paragraph meaning.

That there was no improvement with age in the comprehension of meaning expressed in paragraphs is significant and central to the problem of language mastery by the deaf. As Goodman (*6*) indicates, reading is a complex process which involves the reconstruction of meaning encoded in written language. Its purpose is the comprehension of meaning intended by the writer. Comprehension results from the reader's active sampling from and hypothesis testing on the three categories of cue systems which reside in English: graphophonic cues arising from the relationship of sounds (phonemes) and their written symbols (graphemes); syntactic cues arising out of the arrangement or order of words; and semantic cues which reside in the meanings of the words in a passage. More proficient readers rely less on graphophonic cues and more on syntactic and semantic cues than less proficient readers in extracting the meaning from written material. It is precisely in the areas of word meaning—particularly idiomatic, figurative and abstract—and syntax that the deaf have been found to be deficient. For example, Quigley et al. (15) found that the syntactic rules of standard English were not well established even in eighteen year old subjects. Only simple transformations such as negation, question formation, and conjunction were mastered and then not completely so. Quigley et al. speculate that the deaf may perceive of English as a linear rather than as a hierarchial structure. For example, they may impose a subject-verb-object pattern on sentences in which this order does not apply, or they may connect the nearest noun and verb phrases. In any case, the deaf do not have access to syntactic and semantic cues to the degree that the hearing do. The deaf child, like the less proficient reader, has to rely on the less efficient graphophonic cues. Hartung (11) found no difference between deaf and hearing seven and one-half to nine year olds in the kind of visual perception skill necessary for use of graphophonic cues. More than fifty years ago, Gates and Chase (3) found deaf children to be superior to hearing children in the word perception skills used in spelling. Yet, their relative inability to utilize semantic and syntactic cues may contribute to the low ceiling of about fourth grade level obtained by so many deaf persons in reading achievement.

There are probably other contributing and confounding factors as well. For one thing, the impact of a deaf child in a hearing family (90 percent of deaf children are born with hearing parents) is great. The natural, spontaneous verbal interplay between mother or other caregiver and the infant and toddler is often sharply curtailed or absent altogether. Gross (7) found that mothers of deaf children used less praise and more verbal antagonism than mothers of hearing children. Under such conditions, the child is not stimulated to continue exploration with its vocal mechanism. Continued linguistic development may be impeded in a linguistically neutral or negative environment.

Traditional deaf education practices have been cited by Furth (5) and Kohl (12) as contributing to the retarded language development of deaf children. The oral method of teaching the deaf to speak emphasizes lipreading, learning sound elements and combinations, phonetic spelling, and reading orthographic forms of English. This has been the predominant mode of teaching language to the deaf in the United States. It is hypothesized that its major appeal lies in the assumption that it can teach the deaf to speak. What has always stigmatized the deaf is not their inability to hear but their inability to speak. To speak, to communicate in oral language is taken as a sign of human intelligence. Not to be able to speak is to be cast in with the lot of those who are less than human. Animals are called dumb because they cannot speak, so are the deaf who have not mastered oral communication. It is no coincidence that, for many centuries, the deaf were classed with the insane and retarded.

Despite many years of instruction in the oral method (or some variation of it), a natural sign language persists as the most popular means of communication among the deaf themselves. Even in schools or programs where signing is expressly prohibited, one can observe children using this technique to communicate among themselves. Interestingly, an administrator in a special school for the deaf remarked that it was the most highly verbal children who were most resentful of being prevented from using sign language. Obviously, the deaf themselves find this their most effective means of communication. Furth (5) recommends that parents use a discriminable sign language with their deaf children for the first three years. If parents make a discriminable sign for each word as they speak it, Furth contends, the child will learn the natural language; the child will sign according to English syntax. The signs could be transliterated later to written form for the child to read.

The natural sign language used by the deaf does have some structure and consistency. Yet, it is so context bound, dependent on paralinguistic cues, concrete and subjective (20) that it cannot be as efficient or as sophisticated a mechanism for communication as a true linguistic system. However, the predominance of the oral method is diminishing with the concept that the deaf themselves, or their guardians, ought to be able to decide which system is used. A recent New York State law mandates that a school for the deaf offer more than one teaching methodology so that parents have the option of choice. Today, in addition to the oral method, most schools offer one called total communication which is a combination of the oral and manual (sign) language methods.

Learning to Read

Basic Conditions

There are certain basic conditions which must be met in order to establish the most favorable environment for teaching the deaf child to read. First, teachers must acknowledge honestly their own feelings about hearing-impairment in general and about having a hearing-impaired child in class. It is better to acknowledge feelings even if they are negative, than to attempt to ignore or cover them up. Most teachers will respond with a good bit of anxiety to the idea of a deaf child in class. "Oh no, why me?" may be the response. Teachers, usually already burdened with many responsibilities, may find this just one too many—particularly if they feel lacking in the necessary skills to work successfully with hearing-impaired children. Knowledge is often the best antidote for fear. Teachers should seek out good references on teaching the hearing-impaired, visit a local school for the deaf, enroll in a college course dealing with educating the handicapped, and consult with specially trained personnel (if they are available).

Understanding their own feelings will aid teachers in helping children in the class relate positively to their hearing-impaired classmate. The child's hearing impairment should be acknowledged openly; it should be understood as simply one additional physical feature of the child. Children will be very curious about the child's hearing aid. Its function should be explained simply. The teacher's goal is to establish good peer relationships by removing any mystery which surrounds the hearing-impairment, and by dealing with it openly, honestly, and humanely. Teachers should become quite familiar with the hearing aid apparatus so as to be able to respond to signs of its malfunction. For example, a child's inconsistent behavior might be caused by fluctuating amplification in the hearing aid.

Finally, a child's hearing impairment will necessitate certain simple physical accommodations which soon become habitual. For example, if the child relies primarily on lipreading, Northcott (*13*) advises that you use a natural, clear voice accompanied by normal facial expression. In speaking to the child, face the light or window and stand at a distance of about three feet, positioned at the child's eye level.

Vocabulary Development

The significance of oral language for learning to read, which has been highlighted by psycholinguistic theory, is as valid for the deaf as for the hearing child. However, the understanding vocabulary of several thousand words and the unconscious grasp of the syntactic features of English which we expect to be present in most native speaking first graders, cannot be taken for granted with the deaf child. While experiences to increase vocabulary are a part of all reading programs, they are at the very heart of reading programs for the deaf. As Streng (19) observes, language is the primary concern in teaching deaf children to read.

The development of vocabulary should be a central and continuing activity in each day's plan. Fitzgerald (4) indicates that systematic and consistent training in vocabulary is necessary in each subject and in relation to every activity. The development of vocabulary is begun quite informally when the child first enters school and centers on the child's own personal interests, needs, and activities. The Clarke School (1) advises that formal vocabulary development begin when the child can use some spontaneous language. At this point, daily experiences which are repeated routinely are the ones to which vocabulary is related: recess, snacktime, lunch, library. As the child's interests widen, so does the range of vocabulary development: television programs, vacations, trips, neighborhood. Words are never presented or used in isolation. They are always used in meaningful contexts.

Vocabulary activities include labeling, such as parts of the face, kinds of clothing, or children's names; classifying and categorizing objects, such as sorting plastic tableware by kind and color; pairing synonyms; linking appropriate adjectives with a given noun; classifying verbs according to action, such as movement verbs, sound verbs, feeling verbs; and experiences with words of multiple meanings. For example, to help the child understand the different meanings of the word *make* there should be planned experiences of *making* foods, *making* presents, and *making* constructions out of various artistic media. Subsequently, as speaking vocabulary begins to form the core of reading vocabulary, charts are made to display, illustrate, classify, and categorize new words. In addition, the deaf child's vocabulary development will be facilitated by the presence of hearing peers whose spontaneous language models enrich the verbal milieu.

The significance of the parents' roles in the child's language development should not be underestimated. Teachers will want to develop cooperative relationships with the parents so that home and school can work together to build the child's language function. The Clarke School for the Deaf (1) offers these suggestions to parents: Talk with the child in complete sentences; make a conscious effort to add new words and phrases; have a positive attitude toward the hearing aid, being certain the child wears it all the time, and checking regularly to see if it is in working order; be a good listener, allow the child to express him/herself; tell and read stories aloud; provide meaningful and enjoyable experiences such as cooking and taking trips; provide a positive atmosphere toward reading in the home—let the child see reading being done regularly and routinely by all family members; and visit the public library regularly.

Word Recognition

The first printed words presented to the child should be highly familiar ones which have distinct physical or configuration features. The child should be taught an awareness and recognition of his/her name first as it appears on personal possessions such as a lunchbox or cubbyhole and later as it appears in a sentence that is meaningful to the child. Once the child has mastered its own name, awareness and recognition of classmates' names should be taught. Then the child is introduced to names of family members and pets. From this point, the child is introduced to connected language in meaningful contexts. On completion of an activity, the teacher discusses it and writes a simple descriptive sentence. The child then illustrates the sentence. Familiar words are noted and identified in different settings such as books and filmstrips. Activities to give practice in noticing similarities and differences in visual patterns are begun: matching identical pictures; matching identical letter forms; selecting a word which differs from the others; matching words; associating printed words with pictures; associating printed sentences with illustrations. Words that are mastered should be printed on one inch cards which the child keeps and reviews. These word cards are also used by the child to construct sentences. The manipulation of words as sentence segments into proper positions helps to give the child a visual representation of language structure. As the child gains proficiency in perceiving specific characteristics of printed material, the teacher introduces additional word recognition techniques such as phonics, structural analysis, and phonetic respelling.

Comprehension

Practice in comprehension of spoken language will naturally precede activities designed to improve reading comprehension. For example, the teacher makes an oral command, statement, or question to which the child responds. Later the child's response will be to a written command, statement, or question. The child will work with picture stories, first single and subsequently two or three sentence stories. The child selects which picture is illustrative of the story. Or the child physically enacts or dramatizes the meaning of first, a single sentency story and later, two to three sentence stories. To build sentence memory, the child responds to simple commands written and shown on flash cards. To give practice in recalling story sequence, the child rearranges a series of simple illustrations to conform to the correct sequence of events. Or an experience chart can be composed on scrambled sentence strips. The child then rearranges them in the order that the events actually occurred in the experience.

After the child has acquired some skill in literal comprehension of written material, practice at the interpretation level is begun. For example, in order to teach the child to recognize the main idea of a passage, a sequence of activities such as the following may be used: the teacher asks specific questions which the child answers and, from this, the teacher formulates the main idea; then the teacher asks specific questions which the child answers, but in this activity the child formulates the main idea; then the child both asks the questions and formulates the main idea; finally, the child formulates the main idea immediately after reading the story. Variations on this sequence involve having the child read a paragraph and then select or write a title for it. Or give the child a title and have the child compose a story for it.

Problems in comprehension usually arise for the deaf child with the use of more complex reading material which is marked by idiomatic and figurative language and sophisticated syntax. As noted earlier, it is precisely in these domains that the deaf child's language is deficient. Some believe as Streng(19) does, that mastery of reading material at the intermediate level and above by the deaf child requires a planned, systematic program of instruction in the basic structures of English. In any case, the teacher must preview selected reading material very carefully for potential causes of difficulty such as colloquial, metaphoric, and figurative language and then provide the child with direct instruction on these points. The teacher will stress the importance of the verb as the word that directs the action of the sentence. The child will be taught to find the verb in complex sentences or those with unusual word order. The teacher will instruct the child to locate the subject and verb and then think the meaning of the sentence through. It is essential to relate the more complex meanings encountered in intermediate level and above reading material to actual experiences the child can understand. If, for example, the child has difficulty understanding the conditional, the teacher might say, "Remember Jimmy, we said that *if* it doesn't rain, *then* the class can go outside after lunch." This is then related back to the written sentence in question.

Reading Materials

Quill (*16*) cites the following as prerequisites to introducing the deaf child to reading from books: an understanding vocabulary of at least 500 words, a grasp of connected language with some skill in using it, sentence memory, skill in the mechanics of reading such as left-to-right eye progression, and a desire to read. Actually, the teacher will create much of the child's beginning reading material primarily in the form of experience charts and individual booklets. These begin with a single line which is accompanied by an illustration. Gradually, these charts grow to two and more simple sentences which are also illustrated. Most of the early charts will illustrate a single verb, such as:

We *see* stores.
We *see* houses.

Then charts will incorporate sentences with two or more different verbs:

We went to the zoo.
We saw animals.

Later, the charts will begin to incorporate a beginning notion of the paragraph. Even though sentences are still written on separate lines, they now begin to show a clearer relation to each other. For example:

Mary has a new dress.
It is pink and white.
Her new dress is pretty.

Thus, in a rather carefully programed manner, the deaf child is gradually introduced to language of increasing semantic and syntactic complexity.

Because of the deaf child's limited grasp of the semantic and syntactic features of English, reading from books often presents numerous difficulties. The so-called Sanders Reader was prepared by Alexander Graham Bell in 1873 for use by a six year old deaf child because other suitable printed material was not available. There is still a good deal of dissatisfaction with current reading material primarily because of its uncontrolled presentation of syntactic structures. For example, Hargis et al. (*10*) tested the hypothesis that the direct discourse format, which is frequently found in beginning basal reading series, contributes to the reading difficulty experienced by hearing-impaired children at the first grade reading level. To test the hypothesis they randomly selected stories of about 500 words, long conversational and nonconversational, from a popular reading series. Students from the Tennessee School for the Deaf who were reading at first grade level were selected randomly and then randomly assigned to the conversational and nonconversational stories. Results revealed a statistically significant difference in achievement favoring the group using the nonconversational stories. Hargis (9) believes the solution may lie in the use of specially prepared readers which control syntactical structures and idiomatic and figurative elements as well as vocabulary. N. and J. Peters (14) have compiled an annotated listing of materials in reading and other curriculum areas which were selected for their relative ease. The teacher may also find an earlier compilation by Spache (18) to be helpful in locating suitable printed material.

The natural language competence which we rightfully ascribe to most native speaking children cannot be assumed present in the hearing-impaired child. Instead, the hearing-impaired child usually arrives at school with a serious language deficit. A slow, deliberate, and carefully designed instructional program can help to reduce this language deficiency. A reading plan for the deaf is distinguished from a regular teaching program not by qualitative differences, but by quantitative ones. It is characterized by small, systematic, and carefully planned increments in instruction; much review and reinforcement; and the use of materials which control the semantic and syntactic features of the language. But, like any good reading program, it is based on the child's oral language, it uses the child's interests as a source of material, it teaches skills functionally and in context, and it sees comprehension of meaning as the primary function of reading. The hearing-impaired child can learn to read along with the rest of the class.

References
1. Clarke School for the Deaf. *Reading.* Northampton, Massachusetts: The School, 1972.
2. Dale, D.M.C. *Language Development in Deaf and Partially Hearing Children.* Springfield: Thomas, 1974.
3. Gates, A.I., and E.H. Chase, "Methods and Theories of Learning to Spell Tested by Studies of Deaf Children," *Journal of Educational Psychology*, 17 (1926), 289-300.
4. Fitzgerald, M.H. "Reading: The Key to Progress for Deaf Children," *American Annals of the Deaf*, 102 (1957), 404-415.

5. Furth, H.G. *Thinking without Language: Psychological Implications of Deafness.* New York: Free Press, 1966.
6. Goodman, K.S. "Behind the Eye: What Happens in Reading," in K.S. Goodman and O. Niles, *Reading: Process and Program.* Urbana, Illinois: National Council of Teachers of English, 1970, 3-38.
7. Gross, R.M. "Language Used by Mothers of Deaf Children and Mothers of Hearing Children," *American Annals of the Deaf,* 115 (1970), 93-96.
8. Hammermeister, F.K. "Reading Achievement in Deaf Adults," *American Annals of the Deaf,* 116 (1971), 25-28.
9. Hargis, C.E. "The Relationship of Available Reading Materials to Deficiency in Reading Achievement," *American Annals of the Deaf,* 115 (1970), 27-29.
10. Hargis, C.E., et al. "A Criticism of the Direct Discourse Form in Primary Level Basal Readers," *Volta Review,* 76 (1973), 557-563.
11. Hartung, J.E. "Visual Perception Skill, Reading Ability, and the Young Deaf Child," *Exceptional Children,* 36 (1970), 603-607.
12. Kohl, H.R. *Language and Education of the Deaf.* New York: Center for Urban Education, n.d.
13. Northcott, W.H. "Candidate for Integration: A Hearing-Impaired Child in a Regular Nursery School," *Young Children,* 25 (1970), 367-368.
14. Peters, N., and J. Peters. "Better Reading Materials for the Content Areas," *Volta Review,* 75 (1973), 375-387.
15. Quigley, S.P., et al. *Syntactic Structures in the Language of Deaf Children.* Urbana: University of Illinois Press, 1976.
16. Quill, L.C. *Areas of Instruction for Teachers of Children Who Are Deaf.* Champaign, Illinois: Champaign Community Schools, 1959.
17. Resenstein, J., and W.H. MacGinitie (Eds.), *Research Studies on the Psycholinguistic Behavior of Deaf Children.* Washington, D.C.: Council for Exceptional Children, National Education Association, 1965.
18. Spache, G. *Good Reading for Poor Readers.* Champaign, Illinois: Garrard, 1960.
19. Streng, A. *Reading for Deaf Children.* Washington, D.C.: Alexander Graham Bell Association for the Deaf, 1964.
20. Trevoort, B.T. "Esoteric Symbolism in the Communication Behavior of Young Deaf Children," *American Annals of the Deaf,* 106 (1961), 436-480.
21. Wrightson, H.W., M.S. Aronow, and S. Muskovitz. *Developing Reading and Test Norms for Deaf Children,* Test Services Bulletin, No. 98. New York: Harcourt Brace Jovanovich, 1962.
22. Wrightson, H.W., M.S. Aronow, and S. Muskovitz. "Developing Reading Test Norms for Deaf Children," *American Annals of the Deaf,* 108 (1963), 311-316.